Sir John Soane's Greatest Treasure

THE SARCOPHAGUS OF SETI I

Sir John Soane's Greatest Treasure

THE SARCOPHAGUS OF SETI I

JOHN H. TAYLOR

WITH AN ARTICLE BY HELEN DOREY

PIMPERNEL
PRESS LTD
www.pimpernelpress.com

Pimpernel Press Limited
www.pimpernelpress.com

A catalogue record for this book is available from the
British Library.

Typeset in Dante MT and Charlotte Sans

ISBN 978-1-910258-87-3
Printed and bound in China

9 8 7 6 5 4 3 2 1

Contents

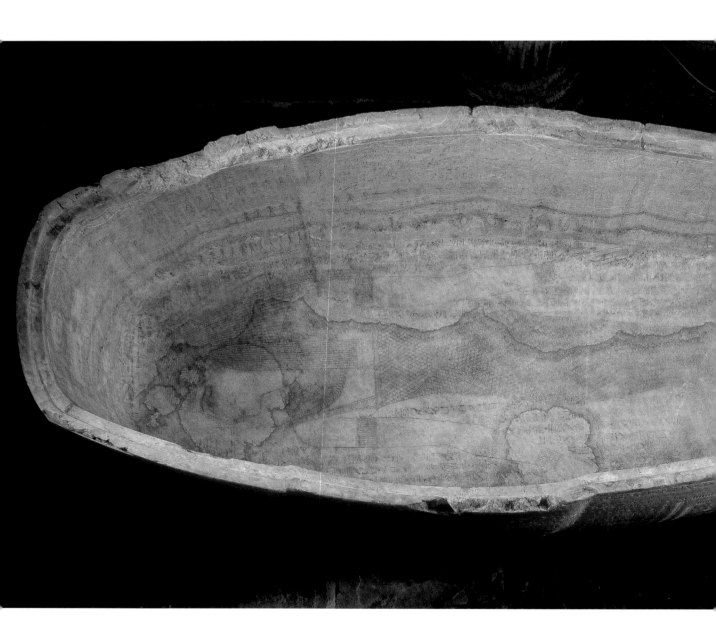

Introduction

The sarcophagus of Seti I, purchased by Sir John Soane in 1824 and installed in the 'Sepulchral Chamber' of his London house, created an instant sensation among all who saw it and became one of the principal treasures of Soane's eclectic collection. It was admired for the exquisite craftsmanship of the carving and the luminosity of the stone, while appealing to the sentiments of the day as a symbol of the vanity of human power and the mystery of the hieroglyphic inscriptions – at that date still undecipherable. Since Soane's time, the birth and growth of the science of Egyptology has illuminated what was dark and has made possible a full and rational interpretation of this celebrated monument. This book sets the sarcophagus in its historical and cultural context, and provides a concise explanation of its complex imagery and inscriptions.

The discovery of the sarcophagus

THE SARCOPHAGUS WAS DISCOVERED by Giovanni Battista Belzoni, one of the most flamboyant personalities in the history of Egyptian exploration. Belzoni (1778–1823), born in Padua, was remarkable both for his enormous physical strength and his aptitude for engineering. Abandoning his performing career in England as a strongman (the 'Patagonian Sampson'), he travelled to Egypt in 1815 in the hope of interesting the Pasha, Mohammed Ali, in his plans for an improved type of water-wheel. This project came to nothing and Belzoni turned his attention instead to the ancient monuments of Egypt. Acting as agent for the British consul general in Egypt, Henry Salt (1780–1827), he used his knowledge of engineering to raise and transport the celebrated granite bust of Ramesses II, known as the 'Younger Memnon', from the king's memorial temple at Luxor to the Nile, eventually to be shipped to the British Museum. Encouraged by this successful venture, Belzoni travelled throughout Egypt between 1816 and 1819, opening the pyramid of Khafre at Giza, clearing and entering the Great Temple of Ramesses II at Abu Simbel, and investigating the Valley of the Kings on the west bank of the Nile at Luxor. The valley contained the rock-hewn tombs of the pharaohs of the New Kingdom (c.1550–1069 BC), many of which had stood open and accessible to travellers since the Roman era. In the hope of finding further tombs there, Belzoni organized excavations in 1817. In this he was very successful, locating eight new sepulchres.

Belzoni surrounded by his discoveries: a version of an engraving by Fabroni commissioned by the explorer's widow Sarah Belzoni in 1824.

Belzoni discovered the entrance to the tomb of King Seti I on 17 October 1817 and entered it on the following day.[1] It proved to be the most magnificent tomb in the valley – a vast sequence of passages and chambers, the walls and ceilings of which were covered with paintings and bas-reliefs of breath-taking beauty. The decoration was, moreover, in near-perfect condition, and 'Belzoni's tomb' (as it was afterwards known) quickly became one of the most visited tourist attractions in Egypt. The tomb had been entered repeatedly in ancient times, and the mummy of the king had been removed, as had most of the burial equipment. Nonetheless, Belzoni found many of the king's *shabti* figures (magical substitutes for the deceased), wooden statuettes of deities, and the mummy of a bull (the presence of which in the king's tomb remains unexplained). But the object which impressed him most was found in the great vaulted burial chamber:

ABOVE LEFT Map of Egypt with inset showing Luxor and the Valley of the Kings.

LEFT Valley of the Kings with the tomb of Seti I in the foreground.

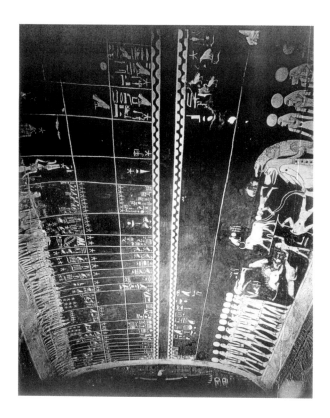

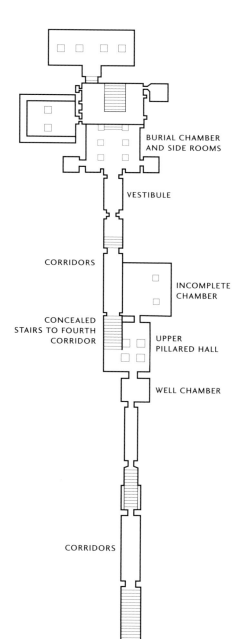

ABOVE Detail of the ceiling of the burial chamber in the tomb of Seti I, showing constellations of the night sky.

RIGHT Plan of the tomb of Seti I.

FAR RIGHT Plan and section through the tomb of Seti I, from *Plates illustrative of the Researches and Operations of G. Belzoni in Egypt and Nubia* (London, 1820–22), pl. 40.

SECTION of the TOMB of SAMETHIS in THEBES.
Discovered and Opened by G. BELZONI, 1818.

'. . . the description of what we found in the centre . . . merits the most particular attention, not having its equal in the world, and being such as we had no idea could exist. It is a sarcophagus of the finest oriental alabaster, nine feet five inches long, and three feet seven inches wide. Its thickness is only two inches; and it is transparent when a light is placed in the inside of it. It is minutely sculptured within and without with several hundred figures, which do not exceed two inches in height . . . I cannot give an adequate idea of this beautiful and invaluable piece of antiquity, and can only say, that nothing has been brought into Europe from Egypt that can be compared with it.'[2]

This wonderful object was found lying over a descending stairway leading to a passage running deep into the hillside. This was not the sarcophagus' original position, but was where it had been left after the removal of the king's mummy by officials who had emptied the tomb of its principal contents about 968 BC. The lid had been taken out and broken to pieces. Belzoni discovered fragments of it at the entrance to the tomb and other pieces were found by later investigators. Belzoni was so delighted by his discoveries that he had casts and facsimile copies made of the tomb's wall-decoration. These he took to London and used to create a 'replica' of part of the tomb which was exhibited at the Egyptian Hall, Piccadilly, in 1821–22.

OPPOSITE Façade of the Egyptian Hall, Piccadilly, the venue for Belzoni's exhibition in 1821–22. John Soane lecture drawing.

BELOW George Johann Scharf the elder, watercolour showing men with billboards including one advertising the Belzoni exhibition, drawn in 1821 (each figure has its date beneath).

The sarcophagus in England

MOST OF THE OBJECTS which Belzoni had found were added to Henry Salt's collection of antiquities, which in due course was offered to the British Museum. Seti I's sarcophagus was taken to Alexandria and embarked on the frigate *Diana*, which sailed for England in 1821.[3] It was expected that the sarcophagus would be purchased by the British Museum, but unfortunately negotiations did not proceed smoothly, not least on account of the strained relationship between Salt and Belzoni. Salt, while acknowledging Belzoni's exceptional abilities, viewed him as an employee, digging and collecting on his behalf. Belzoni, on the other hand, though financed by Salt, wished to be independent and wanted to receive full credit for the discoveries he had made. Salt had left it to the British government to make 'a fair valuation' of his collection, including the sarcophagus. Belzoni, concerned to protect his own interests in the matter, had earlier concluded an agreement with Salt in which it was stated that 'Sig. Belzoni shall be considered as entitled to one half of the surplus of whatever price may be paid for the said sarcophagus exceeding the sum of two thousand pounds.'[4]

As soon as the sarcophagus reached London, Belzoni appeared on the scene, drawing attention to his financial interest in the piece and stating that he had had an offer of £3,000 for it by 'some speculators from the Continent'.[5] He also requested permission to display the sarcophagus in his exhibition in Piccadilly, before it should be removed to the British Museum. Belzoni seems to have feared that once the sarcophagus was in the Museum he would receive nothing of the sum to which he was entitled, and he managed to delay its unloading from the ship. Ultimately, however, his protestations seem to have been ignored, and the piece entered the Museum in September 1821. Here it attracted considerable attention[6]; John G. Children, of the Museum's Department of Antiquities, analyzed a sample of the blue pigment with which the inscriptions and figures had originally been filled, and was able to establish that copper had been used as the main colouring agent.[7]

Over two years then elapsed, during which the sarcophagus was at the centre of a long and unedifying series of negotiations and recriminations over the sale of Salt's antiquities. Although Salt had initially been encouraged by the naturalist Sir Joseph Banks to collect Egyptian artefacts for the national collection, Banks had subsequently changed his attitude. The Museum Trustees (of which Banks was one) showed little enthusiasm and considerable reluctance to accept the Egyptian collection. A major bone of contention was an unrealistically high estimate of the value of the antiquities, which Salt had sent in a private letter to William Hamilton in 1818 and which Hamilton had injudiciously submitted to Sir Joseph Banks. Although Salt repeatedly assured the Trustees that the estimate had been merely a rough guess, never intended as a guide for the government in fixing a price, the document's contents had prejudiced the entire proceedings. Eventually, the collection was purchased by the Museum for £2,000 – considerably less than the sum Salt had spent in amassing it. The sarcophagus, however, was rejected, 'on account of the very high value put upon it by Mr Belzoni'.[8]

In spite of the Museum's refusal to buy the sarcophagus, there was still a considerable body of opinion which favoured its retention – not least on grounds of national pride. If it were retained, the Right Honourable Charles Yorke declared in January 1824, 'this country will be spared the *shame* of having it sent to a foreign Collection after being in *English possession*.'[9]

The sarcophagus, however, was ultimately to find a home in London after all. John Soane had displayed a keen interest in Belzoni's discoveries. Soane attended the exhibition at the Egyptian Hall in 1822, purchased

the publications in which Belzoni described his explorations, and also kept press cuttings about the discovery of the sarcophagus.[10] Among Belzoni's companions when the tomb was found was Henry William Beechey, secretary to Henry Salt. Beechey's father, Sir William, was one of Soane's closest friends, and the connection may have been influential in developing Soane's involvement. The sarcophagus, in particular, seems to have held a strong fascination for Soane. He approached the British Museum through George Booth Tyndale, a trustee of the museum who happened to be renting the house adjacent to Soane's at the time and, early in 1824, he offered to purchase the sarcophagus at the asking price of £ 2,000.[11] A final clear rejection of the piece by the British Museum in April 1824, and the report of Belzoni's death in Africa, which

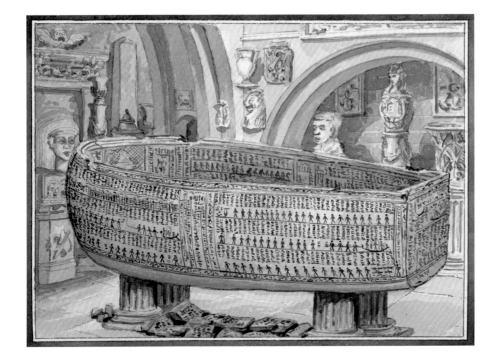

View of the sarcophagus in the centre of the Sepulchral Chamber, preparatory watercolour *c*.1829, for the engraving published in Soane's *Description of the House and Museum . . . of John Soane*, 1830.

View of part of the Collection of Antiquities — from the head of the Soros. —

had occurred in the previous December, removed any remaining obstacles, and Soane's offer was accepted.[12]

The news that Soane had bought the sarcophagus was received with enthusiasm and nationalistic fervour in the London press. The *Morning Post* of 22 April 1824 noted:

> *We believe that there is no country in Europe which would not be proud of possessing such a rarity and that the Emperor of Russia, in particular, would rejoice to obtain it, if it were possible to purchase it from the liberal and patriotic individual who is now its proprietor.*

The sarcophagus was duly installed in Soane's house in Lincoln's Inn Fields on 12 May.[13] Since the door was too narrow to admit it, 'a wide opening' had to be made at the back of the house, and ropes were used to lower it into place in the basement, below Soane's 'Dome' in a space named 'The Sepulchral Chamber' in its honour.[14] It formed a perfect centrepiece for the 'crypt' of Soane's museum, which aptly reflected his self-confessed 'melancholy and brooding' personality.[15]

In 1825, Sarah Belzoni, the explorer's widow, was planning an exhibition in Leicester Square on behalf of Belzoni's family in Padua, and wished to repurchase the sarcophagus to feature as the main attraction. Soane politely disabused Sarah of the notion that he was under any obligation to return the sarcophagus, but he took the opportunity to hold three extravagant receptions at his house on 23, 26 and 30 March.

LEFT Joseph Michael Gandy, view of the head end of the sarcophagus in the Sepulchral Chamber, watercolour dated 9 September 1825.

RIGHT J.M. Gandy, View from the Basement West Corridor looking into the Sepulchral Chamber, watercolour dated 25 July 1825.

July 25. 1825.—
View towards the North side of part of the Collection of Antiquities with the Soros

Ostensibly, these occasions were intended to promote the Leicester Square exhibition, but of course they also served to celebrate Soane's own collection, and the sarcophagus in particular. Over 890 guests were invited, representing the cream of fashionable and cultural society. The ground-floor and basement rooms were illuminated by lamps and candles, carefully positioned to produce a suitably romantic effect. The sarcophagus, glowing in a reddish light cast by shaded lamps, drew much attention.

Benjamin Robert Haydon, who was present at one of the receptions together with the poet Samuel Taylor Coleridge and the painter J.M.W. Turner, recalled:

Fancy delicate ladies of fashion dipping their pretty heads into an old mouldy, fusty, hierogliphicked coffin, blessing their stars at its age, wondering whom it contained and whispering that it was mentioned in Pliny. . .. Just as I was beginning to meditate, the Duke of Sussex, with a star on his breast, and an asthma inside it, came squeezing and wheezing along the narrow passage, driving all the women before him like a Blue-Beard, and putting his royal head into the coffin, added his wonder to the wonder of the rest.[16] (For a longer extract from his description see p. 89-90).

July 29. 1825
View of part of the West End, shewing the broken cover on the Saros.

LEFT J.M. Gandy, view of the sarcophagus in the Sepulchral Chamber looking west, with a partial reconstruction of the lid in place, watercolour dated 17 July 1825.

RIGHT J.M. Gandy, side elevation of the sarcophagus with a conjectural placing of lid fragments at one end, watercolour dated 11 November 1825.

The sarcophagus was placed on display in the centre of Soane's crypt, supported on four truncated fluted columns. A stool, positioned at the head end, enabled visitors to look inside.[17] At first, the fragments of the lid were simply laid on the floor between and around the column-supports, but this was hardly satisfactory, and around 1825 an attempt seems to have been made to reconstruct the lid. Without a model for guidance any attempt to re-create the arrangement of the relatively few surviving fragments was a daunting challenge. To add to the confusion, Soane had also acquired a piece of Seti's canopic chest (the container for the mummified internal organs of the dead king).

Carved from calcite, it was at first thought to be part of the lid of the sarcophagus and was incorporated into the hypothetical reconstructions.[18] Drawings made in the 1820s by Joseph Gandy show the sarcophagus on display, and some of these illustrations appear to show the lid reconstructed.[19] If this reconstruction was actually made, it was short-lived.

In 1863, the fragments of the lid were mounted in plaster of Paris within glazed wooden frames in a conjectural arrangement by the Egyptologist Joseph Bonomi, Curator of Sir John Soane's Museum 1861–78. These frames were at first located under the arches on each side of the sarcophagus. They were suspended

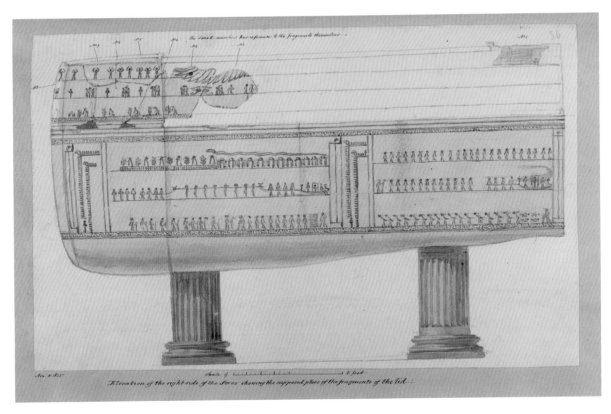

LEFT Charles Martin, portrait of Joseph Bonomi with the sarcophagus, 1867.

BELOW Fragment of the calcite canopic chest of Seti I.

from bars on a mechanism which allowed them to be rotated for inspection. In 1889–90 they were transferred to the West Chamber, a former coal cellar under the next-door house that was incorporated into the basement of the Museum at that time – it was probably then that the wooden frames were mounted on revolving bases.[20] In 1866 the sarcophagus itself was installed in a specially designed glass case with a metal frame, constructed in two parts and mounted on wheels to facilitate its opening.

During the later nineteenth century, the sarcophagus continued to be a focus of interest. An exceptionally accurate facsimile of the decoration was published by Joseph Bonomi and Samuel Sharpe in 1864

(some of the illustrations used in this book are adjusted versions of theirs). In 1908 a new descriptive handbook to the sarcophagus was written by Sir E.A. Wallis Budge of the British Museum.

BELOW J.M. Gandy, *Elevations and sections* of the sarcophagus, the one second from left with a partial reconstruction of the lid in place, watercolour dated 6 November 1825.

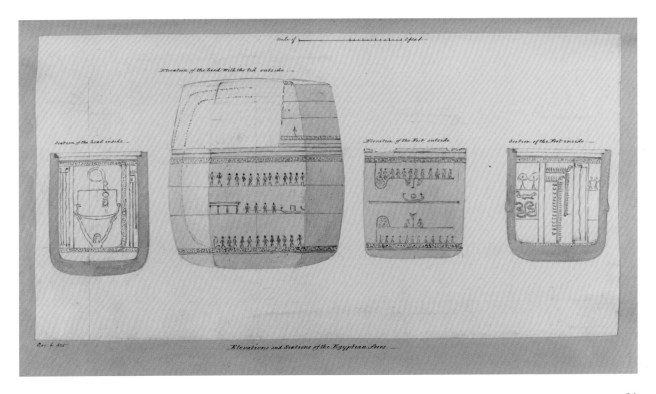

Seti I (*circa* 1290–1279 BC)
His reign and monuments

T HE SARCOPHAGUS WAS NOT, in fact, mentioned by Pliny; nor was it the coffin of Alexander the Great, as some early nineteenth-century commentators had supposed. It was made about 1280 BC to contain the mummified body of the pharaoh Seti I of the 19th Dynasty.[21] Seti was one of the most energetic rulers of the New Kingdom, the period of ancient Egypt's greatest prosperity. His reign was marked by the re-establishing of Egyptian authority in the Levant and the creation of some of the finest architectural and artistic works ever produced in ancient Egypt.

Seti was the son of an army commander named Paramessu, who belonged to a family of military officers which originated in the area of Khatana-Qantir in the eastern Nile Delta. Paramessu enjoyed a dazzling career under Horemheb, last pharaoh of the 18th Dynasty, rising from the rank of an infantry officer to become vizier (chief minister) and then 'King's Deputy' and 'Regent'. Through the granting of these exceptional titles Horemheb, who left no male issue, clearly designated Paramessu as his successor. Besides his personal qualities, Paramessu doubtless recommended himself to Horemheb because he already had a son and grandson – the future kings Seti I and Ramesses II. The existence of this ready-made dynasty offered the prospect of continuity of power and consequent stability for Egypt.

At Horemheb's death Paramessu, dropping the first element from his name, ascended the throne as

Granodiorite statue of Seti I kneeling to present offerings to Osiris. From Abydos, height 115cm (45¼in).

Ramesses I. He was probably advanced in age, and his reign was brief, lasting less than two years. Seti was already a capable and responsible adult by the time of his father's accession, and he exercised many of the duties of the king on Ramesses' behalf, including the leading of military expeditions.

The names and formal epithets chosen for Seti's own royal titulary at his accession clearly indicate that he desired that his reign should be perceived as the dawn of a new era of prosperity for Egypt. He lost no time in initiating an active foreign policy, with the principal aim of reasserting Egyptian authority in Western Asia. By the beginning of the fourteenth century BC, Egypt had gained control of the whole of Palestine, and 'Canaan' – the coastal strip south of the Orontes river, including the important city-states of Byblos, Beirut, Tyre, Sidon and Ugarit. The cities of Qatna and Kadesh, east of the Orontes, were also Egyptian possessions, as were Upe, Damascus and the fertile region of Amki, further south. Egyptian authority in this region gave the pharaohs control of the overland trade routes via Palestine, and major influence in the seaborne commerce of the eastern Mediterranean.

Egypt's chief rival for control of central Syria was the kingdom of the Hittites (Hatti) in central Anatolia. In the late fourteenth century BC, Hittite expansion into northern and central Syria brought the frontiers of Hatti and Egypt into contiguity, and the two superpowers became opponents in the contest for Syrian domination. Within a few years, Ugarit and Amurru, the northernmost of Egypt's Syrian provinces, defected to the Hittites, who also seized Kadesh. Egyptian attempts to recover Kadesh by force were unsuccessful and an uneasy peace was concluded.

With the ascendancy of Seti I there emerged a stronger, more positive policy on the part of Egypt. Active military intervention was conducted on a much larger scale than before, with the aim of recovering the former Syrian possessions. The pharaoh himself took the field, even in quite minor campaigns, something which probably no Egyptian king had done for over one hundred years; this was a clear indication to Palestinian rulers of the determination which characterized the new regime.

Episodes in Seti's military initiatives are recorded in a vivid series of commemorative reliefs, carved

Map of Egypt and the Near East showing the areas of Seti's military activity.

on the north exterior wall of the Hypostyle Hall at the temple of Karnak, and are alluded to in other contemporary sources. The exact chronology and sequence of events are not entirely clear, but a plausible reconstruction of the king's strategy and campaigns can be made. Seti began his operations by securing the route north through Palestine. He had already gained experience of campaigning there on behalf of his father, and in the first year of his sole rule (about 1290 BC) he launched an expedition to subdue the Shasu, nomadic tribes who were causing disturbance along the coastal road from Egypt. This war was swiftly followed by further activity in Palestine. The ruler of Hammath had seized Beth Shan, which had been an important Egyptian garrison-town. Seti sent three divisions of his army simultaneously to Hammath, Beth Shan and Yenoam, and all three towns were taken on the same day. The commemorative reliefs at the temple of Karnak show the Egyptian troops attacking Yenoam, and Lebanese chiefs, having submitted to Seti, being made to cut wood for the barque of the god Amun in his presence.

Further campaigns during the next two to three years consolidated the Egyptian hold on Canaan and the ports of the Phoenician coast. The culmination of Seti's northern wars was his conflict with the Hittite empire, and his recovery of the former Egyptian possessions of Kadesh and Amurru. One of Seti's reliefs at Karnak shows the Egyptian attack on the city of Kadesh, a crucial point on the important commercial routes of the region. The city fell and a victory stela was set up there, a fragment of which still survives. The evidence of the Karnak reliefs indicates that Seti also conquered

BELOW LEFT AND MIDDLE Scenes carved in relief at Karnak, depicting two of Seti's military expeditions: above, the campaign against Yenoam, showing (left) Seti seizing Asiatic captives and (right) presenting prisoners to the Egyptian gods; below, the campaign against the Shasu, with (left) Seti in his chariot and (right) prisoners brought to the frontier fortress of Tjaru, with its boundary canal filled with crocodiles.

BELOW RIGHT Seti ceremonially smiting enemy captives before Amun-Re, who extends a sword towards the king.

Columns in the Hypostyle Hall, Temple of Amun-Re, Karnak.

Amurru at this time and brought it back into the sphere of Egypt's influence. Probably in consequence of Seti's actions, there was a direct clash between the Egyptian and Hittite forces, as recorded in the Karnak reliefs. The accompanying inscriptions, bombastic and stereotyped, do not enable details to be ascertained, beyond the fact that the conflict took place within Hittite territory.

Egypt, however, was unable to retain her distant provinces for long, and Kadesh and Amurru soon fell back under the authority of the Hittites. They were a more powerful foe than any that Seti's predecessors had faced in the struggle for the control of northern Syria, and the two powers seem wisely to have accepted a compromise, probably cemented by a treaty. Egyptian authority was recognized in Canaan and Upe and in the southern ports of the Phoenician coast, while claims to

Kadesh and Amurru were probably relinquished. In thus confining his territorial ambitions within the limits of what could be comfortably retained, Seti showed sound judgement and foresight.

Seti I also waged war against the Libyans on Egypt's western border, and in Nubia to the south. Records of the Nubian campaign describe how the king was in Thebes when a messenger arrived, announcing rebellion in the region of six 'wells' in the land of Irem. An army was sent, and the revolt suppressed, with over 400 men, women and children taken prisoner. This was a small-scale event, aimed at securing Egyptian control of the trade route to sub-Saharan Africa and the gold-bearing regions of Nubia. It was also a source of manpower, the captives probably becoming slaves.

An enormous amount of construction was completed and planned during Seti's reign. All the major administrative and religious centres in Egypt received attention, and the king's projects were supported by the intensification of mining and quarrying activities.

In the Nile Delta, Seti's family homeland, he founded at Khatana-Qantir the palace which was to become the principal residence of the kings of the 19th and 20th Dynasties. This site was ideally located to serve as a military base for campaigns into the Levant, and it included a large industrial complex focusing on the production of armaments and the housing of chariots.

At the ancient royal residence city of Memphis, close to modern Cairo, Seti built a large temple (perhaps a hypostyle hall) dedicated to the god Ptah, besides a memorial temple and a chapel. Most of these structures were subsequently destroyed, and are known today chiefly from small fragments and written references. There were also substantial additions to the great temple of Re at Heliopolis, the principal cult-centre of the sun-god. None of the buildings survive *in situ*, but a votive model commemorating the work indicates that

Osiris enthroned, accompanied by Isis, facing the goddesses Maat and Renpet. Relief carving in the second hypostyle hall of the temple of Seti I at Abydos.

Seti erected a pylon gateway and court, with obelisks, colossal statues and sphinxes. One of these very obelisks, 23m (75½ft) in height, was later transported to Rome, and now stands in the Piazza del Popolo. Other elements of Seti's Heliopolitan structures, including obelisks, statues and offering tables, were moved to Alexandria in late antiquity; some have turned up among the ruins there, and others have been located on the sea bed adjacent to the modern harbour.

Seti I's most imposing monument was the temple he erected at Abydos. This important religious centre was the burial place of the earliest kings of Egypt and the cult centre of the god Osiris. Seti devoted huge resources to his constructions at this site. In Nubia and the eastern desert he exploited and regulated the gold mines and their workforces on behalf of this temple, and a series of royal decrees protected its revenues from official interference and corruption. The temple was built of limestone, on a unique L-shaped plan, and is unusual in having seven distinct sanctuaries dedicated to the gods Amun, Osiris, Isis, Horus, Re-Horakhty and Ptah, and to Seti I himself. An adjacent gallery to the south contains an important list of 76 of the principal kings of Egypt, from the semi-mythical 'Menes' (traditionally held to be the founder of the state) to Seti I. Most of the temple was built of fine limestone, and the walls were decorated with scenes in raised relief. Exceptionally high standards of work were required of the sculptors; in addition to the very fine carving of figures and texts, internal detail of costumes and jewellery (usually added in paint) was here carved in relief as well.

In addition to this temple, Seti executed or planned other works at Abydos, including a highly unusual monument, known as the Osireion. Hidden under a natural or artificial hill planted with trees, this monument was built in sandstone and granite on a layout which recalls that of a royal tomb. The principal chamber contains a sandstone platform surrounded by a channel which could be filled with subsoil water. On this platform are emplacements for a sarcophagus and a canopic chest to hold the mummified viscera of the deceased. The exact purpose of the monument is uncertain, though it is evident that it is both a model of the tomb of Osiris and a representation of the cosmos – the waters symbolizing the watery chaos of Nun, and the superstructure representing the primeval mound on which the creator god arose to fashion the universe. The Osireion has been interpreted as a secondary tomb or 'cenotaph' for the king.

At Thebes, the principal religious focus of Egypt in the New Kingdom, Seti's architects were responsible for some of the most imposing structures still visible today. Chief among these was the great Hypostyle Hall in the temple of Amun-Re at Karnak. This vast monument measures 102 x 53m (334¼ x 174ft) and the roof was supported by a forest of 134 columns. The hall itself was completed in Seti's reign and the decoration on the walls and columns was well under way by the time of his death. They were finished in the reign of Ramesses II. Particularly striking are the reliefs on the external walls on the northern side (mentioned above), which depict episodes from Seti's foreign military operations in graphic detail. In his last years the king had also ordered obelisks and colossal statues from the granite quarries at Aswan for installation at the nearby temple of Luxor. These additions were completed and inscribed by Ramesses II.

On the Theban west bank at Qurna a memorial temple was built to serve the cult of the deified king. Seti's tomb in the Valley of the Kings was one of the largest ever constructed for a pharaoh. It comprised a series of passages and chambers extending 136m (446ft) into the hillside and descending over 100m (328ft) from the entrance level. It was, moreover, the most completely decorated of the tombs, all the walls being covered with painted bas-relief in workmanship of the highest standard. It represents the culmination of a rich, evolving tradition of rock-cut tombs designed for the Egyptian rulers, and to achieve it, Seti augmented and reorganized the community of royal tomb builders who were based on the west bank in the village of Deir el-Medina.

Many other sites in Egypt and Nubia benefited from Seti's attention. Several monuments were erected in the vicinity of mines and quarries, which were intensively exploited in this reign. Seti made two visits to Kanais in the Wadi Abbad, on the route to the gold mines of the eastern desert. He had a settlement for miners built there, together with a small temple, and an inscription describes how the king commanded that wells be sunk to prevent the miners dying of thirst. Further afield, in Sinai, Seti's labourers worked the turquoise mines and began exploiting the copper mines of Timna.

Besides originating new constructions, Seti actively restored temple reliefs throughout Egypt, which had been defaced on the orders of the 'heretic' king Akhenaten in the late fourteenth century BC. Many of these restorations seem to have been secondary alterations made to restorations done by Tutankhamun, and were designed to suppress the memory of that king, who was regarded by posterity as tainted by the heresy of his father Akhenaten.

The exact length of Seti's reign is uncertain, but it probably lasted no more than a decade. While most Egyptologists have assigned him eleven years as king, there are reasons to suppose that he may have died as early as his ninth year. [22] Nothing is known of the

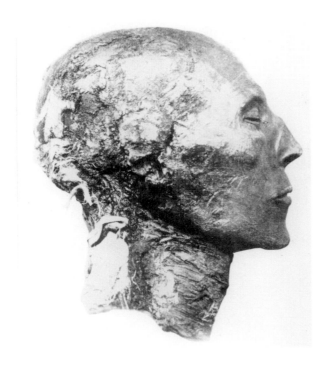

Mummified head of Seti I.

cause or circumstances of his death, but a number of inscriptions show that Seti began grooming his son Ramesses II for kingship while he was still a child. In his own inscriptions, Ramesses claimed that, as heir apparent, he acted in a supervisory capacity in military affairs and in the performance of public works. He even asserted that he had been crowned in his father's own lifetime and provided with a separate household of his own, though these claims may be exaggerated.

Following Seti's death, his corpse was mummified, a process which traditionally occupied a period of seventy days. At the end of that time the linen-wrapped body, adorned with a gold mask and enclosed within its coffins

would have been transported to the king's tomb, to the accompaniment of extensive rituals, and placed inside the calcite sarcophagus, which was probably already installed in the burial chamber. This and the other rooms in the tomb would have been filled with statues, furniture, provisions and magical items to ensure the dead king's safe passage into the afterlife. Finally, the tomb would have been sealed and its entrance probably hidden beneath rubble.

The king's tomb was entered twice in the eleventh century BC, first under the high priest of Amun Herihor, and again in the reign of King Smendes I. These events may have been intended to repair damage following robberies, or they may have been connected with the dismantling of the royal burials in the Valley of the Kings which occurred at that period of economic stress. This 'decommissioning' of the pharaonic cemetery involved the rewrapping of the mummies and the removal of valuables, which were then appropriated by the state, followed by the grouping of the royal mummies in a few easily-guarded tombs or caches. As part of this process, the mummies of Ramesses I and II were brought into Seti's tomb. After another rewrapping, Seti's mummy was removed from his tomb in year 10 of King Siamun (*c.* 968 BC) and secreted in the older tomb of Queen Inhapy. Finally, in the reign of Shoshenq I (*c.* 945–924 BC), the mummies of both Seti I and Ramesses II, together with others, were transferred to a hidden tomb at Deir el-Bahri, where they remained undisturbed until the late nineteenth century AD.

The Deir el-Bahri cache of royal mummies was discovered by members of the local Abd el-Rassul family in the 1870s, and officially cleared in 1881. All the mummies were transported to Cairo, where most of them, including that of Seti I, were unwrapped. The head was extremely well preserved, giving a clear impression of the king's appearance in life.[23]

The sarcophagus
Description, style and function

THE SARCOPHAGUS IS MADE from a single block of calcite, a stone more popularly (but erroneously) known as Egyptian alabaster. This fine stone, the principal source of which was at Hatnub in Middle Egypt, was used extensively for statuary and vessels, but sarcophagi of calcite were rare. Besides the case of the sarcophagus, Sir John Soane's Museum also houses sixteen fragments of the lid which were found in the tomb by Belzoni, as well as two small pieces discovered at its entrance in 1906, which were acquired and presented by Professor Alfred Wiedemann of Bonn. Other pieces of the lid are in the British Museum and the Institut d'Égyptologie in Strasbourg, and recent excavations by the University of Basel and the American Research Center in Egypt have recovered many more from the area between the entrance to Seti I's tomb and that of Ramesses X, which lay immediately to the south-east. Some of these small pieces bear identifiable portions of the sections of the *Book of Gates* which were carved on the

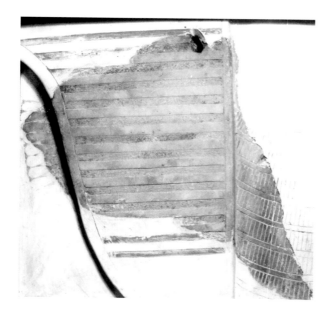

LEFT Fragment of the lid (the darker area of the image), showing part of the royal headdress and collar.

ABOVE Fragments of the lid presented to Sir John Soane's Museum by Prof. Wiedemann in 1910.

exterior of the lid and a few join with fragments in the Soane Museum – yet over 80% of the lid still remains unaccounted for.

The case measures 283cm (111½in) in length and 108cm (42½in) width, and has a thickness of 5.4–6cm (2¼–2½in). Traces of a copper alloy survive on the joining surfaces of the lid and case. These probably formed part of a metal cladding to protect the vulnerable edges of the fragile calcite when manoeuvring the lid into place. Whereas the lid of the sarcophagus was broken into many pieces, the case survived almost intact. There are, however, some areas of damage along the edge, which probably resulted from the levering off of the lid when the mummy was extracted. On the thickness of the case, at the foot end, the name of Belzoni is visible, inscribed in capital letters (curiously, the N is inscribed in reverse).

The general shape of the coffin imitates that of the dead king in his transfigured form, swathed in mummy-wrappings like the god Osiris, and adorned with royal attributes. The contours of shoulders and elbows are indicated in three dimensions, and the knees and the shrouded feet would have been sculpted on the lid, but are now lost. The head of the king was carved on the lid in fully three-dimensional form. The face (now lost) was framed by a royal headcloth, the striped *nemes*. Over this, falcon wings were represented on each side of the face; these wings belonged to some figure now entirely lost, which might have been a goddess or the sun-god in his morning-form as the scarab beetle. On the chest was a bead collar, of which only a small portion survives. The king's hands may also have been represented crossed on the breast, as on the coffins of Tutankhamun, although proof is lacking. All the remaining surfaces of the sarcophagus, both inside and out, were covered with religious texts and images. The central portion of the lid is largely lost,

Belzoni's name incised on the sarcophagus.

The wooden coffin of Seti I, stripped of gilding and inlays and inscribed with notes in hieratic script, recording the official restorations and reburials of the king's mummy in the eleventh and tenth centuries BC.

but the decoration there included at least two large-scale figures of deities with wings extended towards the outer edges of the lid; their precise arrangement and identification remain uncertain. A hieroglyphic inscription around the outer edge of the lid contained addresses to the king by the goddess Nut and the god Thoth. This text is complemented by a similar band of inscription which ran around the lip on the exterior edge of the case, and contained speeches of a series of major funerary deities, ensuring their protection over the dead king. These are the four sons of Horus, who were responsible for guarding the internal organs of the body, two forms of the jackal-headed embalmer-god Anubis, and the sky-goddess Nut herself, whose words express the love she bears to the deceased Seti.

The principal decoration of the sarcophagus consists of a long, illustrated religious text called the *Book of Gates*, which described the journey of the sun-god through the underworld. The images are arranged in a horizontal 'strip'. Sections 1 to 5 were carved on the exterior of the sarcophagus case, beginning on the base of the foot and proceeding from right to left up the proper right side, around the head and down the left side. Sections 6 to 8 were carved on both sides of the lid (exterior) and perhaps originally at the head and foot as well. On account of the fragmentary condition of the lid, section 6 is totally lost, and sections 7 and 8 are incomplete. Sections 9 to 12 were carved on the interior walls of the sarcophagus case. Here the images run from left to right, beginning at the proper left shoulder and culminating at the head end. On the floor of the sarcophagus case is a large figure of the goddess Nut and a selection of religious texts.

Belzoni noted that at the time of discovery the figures carved on the sarcophagus were coloured with a dark blue pigment. A description written in 1825 and drawings made in 1830 indicate that some blue colouring still remained at that period, at least on the lid fragments. Almost all of this has now disappeared, and it remains uncertain how much of the original pigment had survived when the sarcophagus was discovered. The situation was complicated by a misguided attempt at 'restoration'. According to letters received by the Curator from Henry Tompkins in 1889–93, a Mr Hobson, temporary curator of the museum in 1860, 'very improperly occupied his leisure hours with filling in with black paint the hieroglyphics of the very valuable sarcophagus'.[24] Following complaints, the black pigment was removed from the case, but not from the fragments of the lid.

Cleaning of the sarcophagus in 2008 provided an opportunity to apply scientific imaging techniques in order to establish the composition of the original ancient pigment and the extent of its survival. A survey carried out by staff from the British Museum using visible-induced luminescence (VIL) imaging and Raman spectrometry revealed that many small particles of calcium-copper tetrasilicate ('Egyptian blue') survive in the incised figures and hieroglyphs. Through chemical change, these traces of the original colouring matter now appear brown-black when viewed under natural lighting conditions. A more obviously blue colouring which is visible in many places consists of artificial ultramarine, probably added during nineteenth-century restorations. The VIL and Raman survey also showed that Egyptian blue is present not only on the formal designs of the sarcophagus but also in the natural veins and imperfections in the stone, suggesting that the pigment had been applied by smearing it extensively over the calcite surface before removing the excess to leave the blue colouring only on the inscriptions and images.[25]

Seti's sarcophagus represents an innovation in the constantly evolving strategies which the Egyptians adopted to house the mummy of the dead ruler in a protected environment which was also conducive to his resurrection. Since the middle years of the 18th Dynasty (c.1539–1292 BC) the outer casing of the king's body had been a box-shaped sarcophagus of quartzite or granite, containing up to three anthropoid mummy-cases, the outer ones of richly gilded and inlaid wood, the innermost (at least in the case of Tutankhamun) being of solid gold. The sarcophagus of Seti I is the first attested instance of an anthropoid mummy-case in stone being employed for a king's burial. It was a practice which was followed by several later rulers, including Ramesses II and his successor Merenptah, each of whom possessed a similar anthropoid sarcophagus. In Merenptah's tomb the calcite coffin formed the innermost of a series of four sarcophagi, the outer ones being of granite, rectangular in shape but each of different design. Whether Seti I possessed a similar assemblage is unknown; no fragments have been found which could have belonged to such rectangular sarcophagi. But since one of the sarcophagi of Merenptah was taken to Tanis in the Delta for reuse by a later king, and the cases of the others were deliberately broken up to enable the stone to be recycled, the absence of traces of such pieces from Seti's tomb is not conclusive proof that they were not originally present. An alternative possibility is that a wooden sarcophagus was placed over the calcite coffin, though there is no direct evidence for this either.

The sarcophagus (or sarcophagi) would have been located within a series of gilded wooden shrines, like those found in the tomb of Tutankhamun. Within the calcite sarcophagus there must have been at least one coffin of gilded wood and probably an inner one

of solid gold, similar to that of Tutankhamun. Such a sumptuous inner coffin could not, of course, be expected to have survived the attentions of tomb robbers or the 'restorations' of later rulers eager to convert such resources back into usable wealth. However, when the mummy of Seti I was restored and reburied for the first time, at the end of the New Kingdom, it was placed inside a cedar-wood coffin (now in the Egyptian Museum, Cairo, CG 61019) which has been thought by some to have been part of his original burial equipment. Its dimensions would allow it to rest comfortably inside the calcite sarcophagus and in its pristine state it was probably a fine piece of craftsmanship. Its exterior surface was originally gilded, but this had been stripped away and the face remodelled before Seti's reburial, leaving only the beautiful inlaid eyes to hint at its former grandeur. The stripped coffin was given a coating of white paint, and its occupant's names crudely scrawled on the breast. Beneath the cartouches containing Seti's royal names is a series of dockets, written in black ink in the hieratic script, recording the dead king's various rewrappings and reinterments until he reached his final ancient resting-place in the 'Royal Cache' at Deir el-Bahri.

Blue-glazed faience shabti figure of Seti I, from his tomb in the Valley of the Kings. Height 22.8cm (9in).

WEST

Decoration of the sarcophagus

ROYAL FUNERARY TEXTS OF THE NEW KINGDOM

Egyptian conceptions of the afterlife were based essentially on the interrelated mythology of the gods Osiris and Re (or Ra). Osiris was believed to have been murdered by his brother, the god Seth, and later restored to life as ruler of the kingdom of the dead. Re, the creator sun-god, underwent a symbolic death at sunset but was reborn each successive dawn. The stories of both gods served as models for the posthumous rebirth of mortals. During much of the 3,000-year period in which Egyptian funerary mythology evolved the king was distinguished from his subjects in death as he had been in life. By the thirteenth century BC, the pharaoh, like other Egyptians, expected to become identified with Osiris after death, but his immortality depended to a greater degree on his sharing the experience of the sun-god as he traversed the netherworld during the night. This was the dominant theme of the texts and images which were carved and painted on the walls of the passages, chambers and pillars of the pharaohs' rock-cut tombs. Complementary decoration was placed on the shrines and sarcophagi which housed the king's mummy.[26]

The texts in the New Kingdom royal tombs can be grouped into specific compositions, known collectively as the *Books of the Netherworld*. The tomb of Seti I

contains four of them: the *Book of Amduat*, the *Litany of Re*, the *Book of Gates* and the *Book of the Celestial Cow*. The whole of the *Book of Gates* is also inscribed on the calcite sarcophagus. Common to all these works is the theme that the rebirth of the king was to be achieved by linking his fate with that of the sun-god Re, to whom was attributed the creation of the universe. Each new dawn was symbolically regarded as a repetition of the original creation, and it was held to be possible only because the sun-god was himself rejuvenated during his nightly passage from the western to the eastern horizon. This journey took place beneath the earth, in the netherworld ruled over by Osiris.

The principal texts of this genre, the *Amduat* and the later *Book of Gates,* describe each stage in the journey through the hours of the night. After setting in the west each evening, the sun was believed to pass into the subterranean netherworld, or *Duat*, sailing back to the eastern horizon on a waterway which mirrored the Nile on the earth above. This river was Nun, the primeval waters, and to enter this realm was to return to the state of chaos which existed before the creation. During this journey the sun-god experienced rejuvenation, enabling him to emerge like a newborn child into the eastern sky at dawn and so to continue the existence of the created universe. The texts of the *Books of the Netherworld* emphasize the close identification of the dead king with the sun-god. The king thereby would share in the rebirth which the deity experienced. Besides magically conferring eternal life on the dead ruler, these compositions described every aspect of the hidden world of the beyond in repetitious and often obscure detail. The divinities inhabiting the netherworld are depicted and listed, as are the hostile forces who threatened to obstruct the sun-god's journey. The books also illustrate the destinies of the blessed and the damned – those who have and have not lived according to *Maat*, the principle of right and justice; the blessed receive new life and sustenance, while the damned are condemned to torture and destruction.

The architecture of the king's tomb, with its sequence of long and twisting passages, descending deeper and deeper into the earth, was intended to mirror the topography of the netherworld. It was designed as the setting for a conceptual recreation of Re's nocturnal travels. Hence the burial chamber, the focal point of the tomb, was not just the resting place of the dead king; it was also the culmination of the god's journey – the point from which he (and the king) would rise up, reborn, into the sky each dawn. To promote this concept the burial chamber of Seti I's tomb, in which his sarcophagus lay, was a vast hall with a vaulted ceiling, on which were painted the constellations of the night sky.

THE *BOOK OF GATES*

The bulk of the decoration on the sarcophagus of Seti I consisted of the complete text and scenes of the *Book of Gates*. This composition was divided into twelve sections, each corresponding to one hour of the night. Every hour was divided from the next by a schematized depiction of a massive fortified gate, extending almost the full height of the sarcophagus. The notion that the netherworld was accessed through a series of gates is found in several ancient Egyptian sources, including the *Book of the Dead*. The gates were protected by

fearsome guardians, who challenged and questioned the deceased to ascertain that he was worthy to enter the hereafter. The arcane knowledge required to negotiate these obstacles was made available to the deceased in the form of funerary texts; the unrighteous, unequipped with this information, would be excluded from the afterlife. No two of the gates are identical in appearance, but most have standard features. The open leaf of a door is represented, and a giant snake-guardian is shown. Before the open door are two schematically drawn crenellated walls, each crowned with a snake spitting fire. Groups of mummiform gods, divine standards and sceptres also feature, watching over the threshold. The gates themselves have symbolic names such as 'the one with sharp blaze', in reference to the fire-spitting snakes which illuminate the gate for the sun-god to pass through, and ward off hostile forces. The snakes also have terrifying names, such as 'Bloodsucker' and 'He whose eyes spew fire'. Apart from the beginning and end of the composition, the spaces representing the hours are divided into three horizontal bands or registers. The focal point of each scene is the barque of the sun-god, which is towed by human figures along the waterway which flows through the netherworld. The texts explain that as the sun-god's barque approaches each gate the guardians are called upon to open it. The bolts are drawn back and the gates open to admit the god. Then they slam shut, denying access to the hostile forces of chaos.

In the description which follows, the central register is generally described first, since this includes the image of the sun-god, the focus of the narrative. The subordinate images in the upper and lower registers are explained afterwards.

The illustrations of the scenes and inscriptions in Egyptian blue are adaptations by John Bridges of the plates drawn for Samuel Sharpe and Joseph Bonomi, The Alabaster Sarcophagus of Oimenepthah . . ., *London, 1864.*

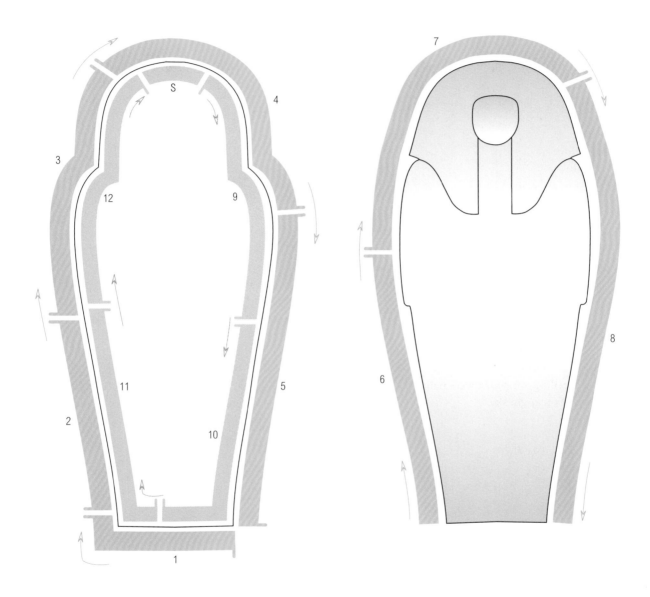

Diagram of the surfaces of the sarcophagus, illustrating the location of the twelve sections of the *Book of Gates* and the concluding scene ('S').

FIRST DIVISION
Exterior of sarcophagus, foot end
(West side in Museum)

This scene represents the western horizon, the intermediary zone between the upper and lower regions where the sun-god begins his nocturnal journey. The western mountain, where the sun sets, is schematically represented above and below by undulating tracts of sandy desert (represented by dotted areas). Enclosed within each zone of the mountain are twelve human figures representing the blessed dead in the netherworld, who greet the sun-god at his approach.

In the centre, between the two banks, is the barque of the god sailing on the netherworld river. The god himself is represented as a scarab beetle within the solar disc, and the image is itself surrounded by a snake with its tail in its mouth. This serpent probably represents Mehen, 'the coiled one', who protects the sun-god during his journey through the netherworld. It is shown around the god's shrine in the later divisions of the *Gates*. At the prow and stern of the barque stand two figures who will accompany the god in all the subsequent stages of his journey; they are Sia (knowledge) and Heqa (magic), the two personifications of his creative power.

On each bank is set a pole, protected by two kneeling divinities called 'Netherworld' and 'Desert', personifications of the realm of the dead. The upper pole has the head of a jackal, that below the head of a ram. Similar ram-headed and jackal-headed poles are depicted in a scene on the second shrine of Tutankhamun and in the later *Book of Caverns*, where

they are referred to as the 'head' and 'neck' of Re. As the accompanying texts make clear, the poles are the physical manifestations of the 'command' of the sun-god which will bring new life to the blessed dead.

Turning from the foot end to the right side of the sarcophagus, one sees the open leaf of the gate leading into the second section of the netherworld, protected by a tall snake named 'Guardian of the desert'. The inscription on the door leaf states that Sia, acting as the sun-god's spokesman, gives the command to this snake: 'Open your door for Re', so that the god's barque may enter and bring light to the darkness beyond. This gateway is much simpler in design than the others in the *Book of Gates*, where the door leaf is protected by a double crenellated wall, and watched over by snakes and mummiform guardians. It is possible that the elaborate depiction of the western mountain, just described, takes the place of these features here.

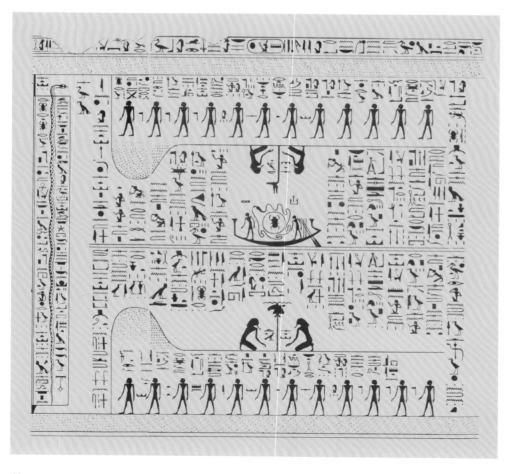

SECOND DIVISION
Lower right exterior of sarcophagus case
(North side in Museum)

On the extreme right in the **central register** is the sun-god's barque, being towed along by four figures identified as 'occupants of the netherworld'. The shape of the barque is essentially the same as in the first hour, but the sun-god himself has taken on a different form, which appears in all the subsequent sections as far as the twelfth hour. He is depicted as a ram-headed man, a form known as the 'Flesh of Re'. He stands within a shrine, around which the Mehen snake – the god's guardian and protector – coils itself. Another snake,

possibly representing the *uraeus* serpent of the king's diadem, appears facing the god inside his shrine.

The barque is confronted by fourteen deities, among whom are Nepen (the personification of 'grain'), Horus and others called 'gods who are at the entrance' (i.e. the approaches to the subterranean netherworld). The text above explains that the sun-god has entered the netherworld 'to hold judgement in the west', to make a just apportionment of offerings, to reward the glorified spirits of the righteous dead, and to punish the damned

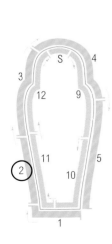

with destruction. The gods who face him declare: 'Darkness rules in the ways of the *Duat* [Netherworld]. Open the closed doors, you Opener of the Earth. . .' By carrying out their wishes, the sun-god dispels the darkness with his light and brings new life to the dead dwelling in the netherworld.

Two groups of twelve figures in the **upper register** represent the righteous dead. The text above explains that they are ones who live according to *Maat*, the ideal state of cosmic order. They worship Re and fight on his behalf against his great enemy, the snake Apophis. In return, they are rewarded with offerings and the assurance that their souls shall not perish. In contrast with these blessed beings, the twenty bound figures in the **lower register** represent the damned, those who have 'spoken evil' and 'done evil' against their

creator. They have been vanquished by the sun-god, and their wretched state is reflected in the manner of their depiction, as captives with their hands tied behind them. At the extreme right is the figure of the god Atum, leaning on a staff and watching over the figures in front of him. In other ancient texts Atum is the personification of the sun at evening, and is often depicted as an old man with bent back and staff. The unity of Re and Atum is alluded to in the text above the figures, yet at the same time they are distinct entities, and to Atum falls the role of restraining and guarding the enemies whom Re has overthrown. He describes the punishment that lies in store for them: they are to be decapitated and their *bas* (spiritual aspects) condemned to non-existence; unlike the blessed dead, they will not enjoy the rejuvenating experience of seeing the sun-god.

Immediately in front of Atum four unfettered figures lie stretched on their backs. They are called 'the Inert Ones' and perhaps represent the four cardinal points of the netherworld, inactive because they have no role to play in the lightless and chaotic region in which the damned are punished.

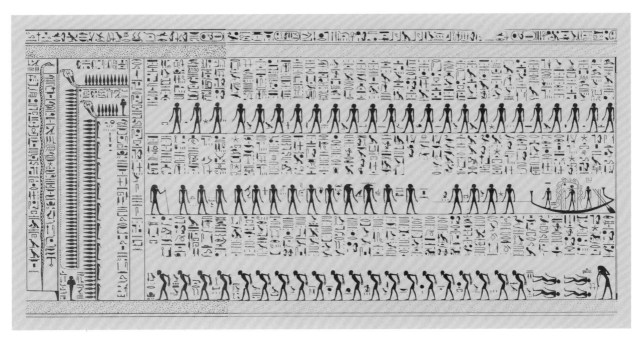

THIRD DIVISION
Right exterior of sarcophagus case
(North side in Museum)

The solar barque passes through the **second gate**, guarded by a snake named 'the Twister', and is then seen at right in the **central register**, towed as before by four 'occupants of the netherworld'. They walk towards a long object with a bull's head at each end, supported on the shoulders of eight standing mummiform figures. This is identified in the text as the 'Earth-barque'; it is intended to encapsulate, in a single image, the whole of the terrestrial netherworld in which the sun-god's nocturnal journey takes place.

On top of the Earth-barque are two bulls and seven squatting mummiform figures who represent the crew of the vessel. The sun-god's boat is shown about to be pulled *through* the Earth-barque (the tow-rope entering the mouth of one of the bull's heads and emerging at the other). Another four 'occupants of the netherworld' are shown holding the tow-rope to the left of the Earth-barque, having already passed through it. They approach four figures shrouded in linen wrappings.

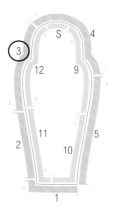

The purpose of this strange scene is to bring about the sun-god's rejuvenation, one of the main themes of his nocturnal journey, and the episode with the Earth-barque has a parallel in a scene in the earlier *Book of Amduat*, where the sun-god and his company become rejuvenated by being pulled through the body of a long snake.

In the **upper register**, at right, protected by a giant snake called 'the Flaming One', are twelve shrines with vaulted tops. Their shutter-like doors are open, revealing that each contains a mummy-shaped figure. These represent the embalmed dead who are about to be awoken from the sleep of death by the appearance of the sun-god. The text above recounts how the closed and darkened shrines are opened and filled with light on the appearance of the god, who brings breath to the noses of their occupants. They in turn rejoice at the god's approach, but this is only a temporary rejuvenation, for when in due course the god passes on to the next division of the netherworld the gates close behind him and darkness returns. The dead give vent to loud lamentations before resuming their former state of inertness.

To the left of the shrines is the Lake of Fire, an elongated shape with rounded ends, filled with stylized ripples of water. Twelve of the blessed dead emerge from it, their heads atop stylized mummiform bodies. Ears of barley, which will provide food offerings for them, are shown growing on its banks. But for the unrighteous, the Lake of Fire is a place of terror. The accompanying text describes its ambivalent nature: 'This lake is filled with barley, but the water of this lake is fire. Birds fly away from it when they see its water and smell the stink which is in it.' While fire is one means of destroying the unrighteous in ancient Egyptian texts, the blessed dead are immune to it, and receive the promise of Re that they will enjoy their proper offerings. For them, the lake provides coolness and nourishment.

In the **lower register**, below the sun-god's barque, stands Atum leaning on his staff, as in the previous hour. At his feet lies the serpent Apophis, the principal enemy of the sun-god, and to the left are nine figures who are named as 'the company who restrain Apophis'. Apophis tries to halt the progress of the sun-god's barque, but is always defeated. The struggle is one of the main themes of *Gates*, and the text of this division alludes to his fate: 'Your head is cut off, Apophis, your coils are cut through . . .Your approach to the boat of

Re does not exist. You shall not descend inimically against the ship of the god.' The text explains that Apophis has been overthrown by Atum and his nine helpers, who are the blessed dead. Further to the left, a second figure of Atum confronts nine 'possessors of offerings', whose role is to drive away evil and to assist in the overthrow of Apophis.

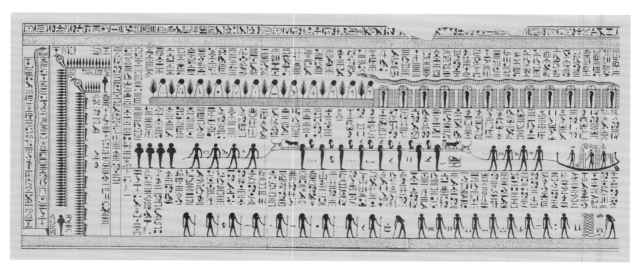

FOURTH DIVISION
Head end and upper left exterior of sarcophagus case
(East and South sides in Museum)

Next comes the **third gate**, and to the left of this, in the **central register**, the solar barque is towed by its attendants towards a large shrine, divided into nine compartments. In each of these lies a mummy. This scene is a further illustration of the theme of the reawakening of the dead, but these mummies, unlike the figures in the third division, lie on their backs awaiting the approach of the sun-god. The inscriptions explain that at the god's command they awake, rise up and stretch themselves. As before, this rejuvenation is only temporary, and the blessed dead wail piteously when the doors close behind the departing god, and they return to their rigid mummy-forms within their shrines.

To the left of the shrines [*left exterior, South side in Museum*] is a curious representation of time. Twelve goddesses standing on sloping platforms personify the hours of the night, each of which constitutes a lifetime for the blessed dead. Between them lies a many-coiled snake representing the infinity of time. The text

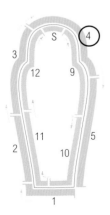

explains that the hours proceed from this snake, only to be swallowed by it when they have run their course. The goddesses of the night-hours, too, play their part in guiding the sun-god forward on his journey.

In the **upper register**, at right, stand twelve 'gods who have gone to their *kas*'. These are more of the blessed dead, who have acted righteously on earth, and their title reflects the hope that the *ka* (a spirit form of the individual) would survive beyond death, to be reunited with the body. An essential condition for this was a supply of provisions for the *ka*, and these are promised in the accompanying text. The figures walk towards two stretches of water, each divided in the centre. The first is called the 'Lake of Life', a place of purification which simultaneously provides life for the righteous while repelling the wicked. The twelve jackal-headed figures who occupy the lake are again representations of the dead. Beyond the Lake of Life is the 'Lake of uraeus-serpents'. This is a fiery region and, like the Lake of Fire, prevents all wrongdoers from approaching. In this case it is the ten serpents upon the lake who, with hissing 'voices' and fiery breath drive the damned away.

The **lower register** and its text alludes to the all-important relationship between Osiris, ruler of the netherworld, and his son Horus. The small figure of Osiris, within his dome-topped shrine [on the curve at the upper left corner of the sarcophagus], is the focal point of the scene. He is confronted by a large serpent, 'the Burning One', and surrounded by an entourage of divine beings. At the extreme right stands Horus, in the place occupied by Atum in the two preceding divisions. The text explains how Horus descends to meet his

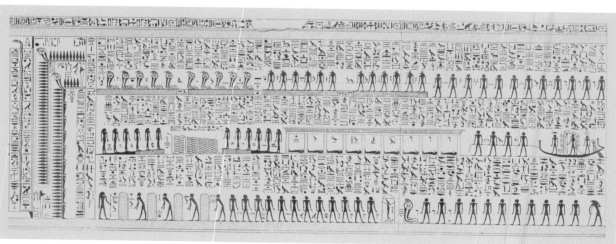

father, to adorn him with the *seshed*-band (a headband which endows him with power), to bring about his transfiguration and to overthrow his enemies. Osiris replies: 'Come to me, my son Horus, in order that you may save me from those who act against me, and in order that you may assign them to him who is in charge of destruction.' This is not simply an allusion to the myth of Osiris, in which Horus supports and protects his father. Horus is here equated with the sun-god, and it is he who is bringing life and protection to Osiris.

At the left extremity of this register are four domed shapes, representing pits set aside for the punishment of the damned. The coloured version of the scene painted on the walls of Seti's tomb shows that the pits were filled with flames, making this image a forerunner of the early Christian concept of Hell. By each pit stands a guardian facing a divine figure whose task is to supervise the destruction of the unrighteous. The text contains Horus' address to the guardians: "You have seized the enemies of my father. You have dragged them to your pits, on account of these [evils] which they have done against the Great One . . ." From this it is apparent that this particular punishment is reserved for the enemies of Osiris.

FIFTH DIVISION
Left exterior of sarcophagus case
(South side in Museum)

After passing through the **fourth gate**, the sun-god's barque is seen in the **central register**, pulled by its four attendants towards nine figures in mummy wrappings who are restraining a large snake, 'the coiling one'. Though not named as such, this snake is probably to be identified as Apophis; it is certainly hostile, for Re commands them to 'hold fast' the serpent so as not to jeopardize his rejuvenation. To the left stand twelve human figures. They represent the *bas* (like the *ka*, the *ba* was a spiritual aspect of human existence) of the righteous, 'who have spoken *Maat* on earth'. The sun-god promises them strength, breath for their nostrils and property in the 'Field of Reeds' – an agricultural paradise in which the dead plough, sow and harvest abundant crops. In addition, Re commends them to 'He who is over his tribunal'. This personage is the figure at the extreme left-hand end of the division. He stands facing the *bas*, who will act as magistrates in the Hall of Judgement which appears in the next scene.

In the **upper register**, at right, twelve figures representing the blessed dead bow to welcome the sun-god,

and to their left are twelve deities carrying a measuring cord, of the kind used by surveyors to measure fields. These twelve gods, supervised by four overseers at the extreme left, have the task of allotting to the blessed dead plots of land in the Field of Reeds for the cultivation of food offerings.

In the **lower register**, at right, is Horus leaning on his staff. In front of him is a series of human figures representing the races of mankind according to ancient Egyptian perceptions. These are, from right to left, four 'Men' (i.e. Egyptians), four Asiatics, four Nubians and four Libyans. In the more detailed painted scenes on the walls of some royal tombs the figures are differentiated by their skin colouring, hairstyles and costumes, but here they are uniformly schematized. The text explains that all these races will enjoy transfiguration through the power of Re. It is interesting that foreign peoples, although traditionally regarded by the Egyptians as their enemies, are here acknowledged as part of the creation of the sun-god, and that they too will find a place in the afterlife. This cosmopolitan attitude (which is foreshadowed in the pharaoh Akhenaten's great hymn to the solar disc) probably proceeded from increased contact between Egyptians and foreign peoples in the New Kingdom.

To the left, twelve gods carry a snake. The hieroglyphic sign for 'lifetime' is inscribed eleven times, between the figures of the gods. Their role is to measure the lifespans of the *bas* (or spirits) of the dead in the hereafter. The duration of their renewed existence in fact is limited to the one hour of each night during which the sun-god is present; the texts make clear, however, that for the dead this 'hour' encompasses an entire human lifetime. Thus, among the dead, the measurement of time runs differently to that in the world of the living. This division is completed by a group of eight entities, at lower left, who assist in the destruction of the sun-god's enemies.

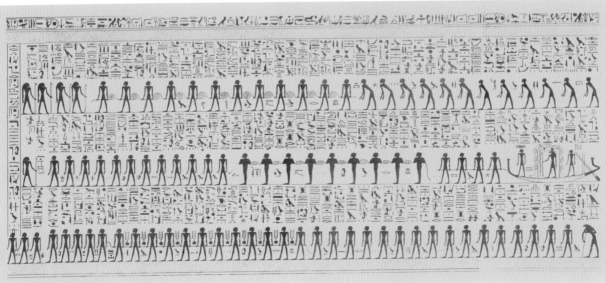

THE FIFTH GATE AND THE JUDGEMENT HALL OF OSIRIS
Lower left exterior of sarcophagus case
(South side in Museum)

In its basic elements, the **fifth gate**, 'Mistress of Lifetime', is similar to the preceding ones, with the usual serpent- and mummy-guardians. The crenellated walls and the open door are, however, widely separated and in the intervening space is a depiction of a judgement scene. A divine judgement in which the deceased had to prove his worthiness to enter the netherworld was a crucial element of concepts of the afterlife in New Kingdom Egypt; in its most familiar form, in the *Book of the Dead*, the dead person's heart is weighed in a balance before Osiris. The judgement scene in the *Book of Gates* has a slightly different function. It is concerned not so much with the vindication of the individual but with emphasizing the distinction between the justified and the damned.

The inscriptions accompanying this important scene are in cryptographic writing, a feature found nowhere else in the *Book of Gates*. It is used here as a means of emphasizing the sacred character of the

text. This unfortunately hampers interpretation, but with the aid of the images the general purport of the scene is clear. The principal figure is Osiris, who sits enthroned on a high dais (centre right). The steps to his throne (rising from the left) are occupied

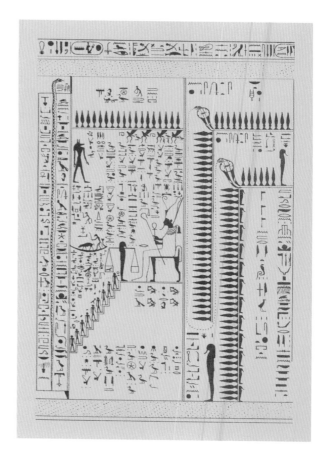

by nine figures of the blessed dead, and directly before the god is the balance of judgement, supported on the shoulders of a mummiform figure. While the blessed face Osiris to receive eternal life, the damned are shown as bound and vanquished captives beneath his throne. The defeat of the forces of evil is also embodied in the figure of a pig in a boat, which is driven from Osiris by a monkey. Above, as though emerging from the heavens, are four inverted antelope heads, sinister guardians who watch over the damned. In the upper left corner stands the god Anubis, the embalmer, who is a regular participant in the judgement of the dead.

This scene is a reminder that it is Osiris who rules in the netherworld kingdom. By vanquishing the damned he makes possible the safe continuation of the sun-god's nocturnal journey. The judgement is deliberately given special focus in the *Book of Gates*. In the tomb of Horemheb (*c.* 1295 BC) the scene is strategically placed on the wall of the burial chamber, directly over the king's sarcophagus. On the sarcophagus of Seti I it marks the end of the decoration on the exterior of the case.

SIXTH DIVISION
Exterior of lid
(Lost)

This section, which would have been depicted on the lid of Seti's sarcophagus, is completely missing, but its content is known from other sources. It depicted the meeting of the sun-god with his own corpse in the deepest part of the netherworld. This reuniting of the god's *ba*-spirit with his body was the culmination of the night journey, and brought about the rejuvenation which all dead mortals hoped to experience. The entrapment of the hostile serpent Apophis is shown, as is a series of mummies lying on a snake-shaped bier in the 'sleep of death', from which they will be awakened by the passage of the sun-god. They are promised light, air and bodily integrity, and freedom from the confinement of their mummy wrappings.

The description of the lid that follows relates to its surviving fragments which are in the collections of Sir John Soane's Museum and elsewhere but which are not on display with the sarcophagus

SEVENTH DIVISION
Exterior of lid, right side

The gate at the conclusion of the Sixth Hour is lost on account of the fragmentary nature of the sarcophagus lid, and large sections at the beginning and end of the Seventh Hour are also missing.[27] In the **middle register**, following the rejuvenating encounter with his corpse, the sun-god's *ba* proceeds on its way in the solar barque. Planted in front of it, and watched over by Atum, is a group of jackal-headed poles, the 'Stakes of Geb'. To each of these two of the damned are tied to be punished. The tying of offenders to a stake for punishment was a feature of the Egyptian penal system and is depicted in tomb scenes as early as the Old Kingdom. The pairs of figures tied to the Stakes of Geb, however, are identified as the enemies of particular gods - Re, Atum, Khepri, Shu, Geb, Osiris and Horus – and before each stands a god appointed to carry out the punishment, which will involve decapitation. The eyes depicted between the first and second stakes are

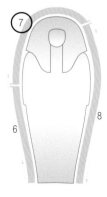

not part of the *Book of Gates*; they are a legacy of the coffin decoration of a much earlier period, when a pair of eyes, painted or carved on the side of the coffin, enabled the occupant to look out by magic and to watch the rising sun at dawn, symbolizing the renewal of life. This feature seems to have been included on Seti's sarcophagus out of respect for an ancient tradition.

The **upper and lower registers** are mainly concerned with the provisioning of the righteous. Above were twelve figures of the blessed dead, each carrying a bread basket on his head, then a further group of twelve (only six survive) in the same pose, with the feather of *Maat* on their heads. According to the text, the first group have not obstructed any of the transfigured dead from receiving life-giving breath or drink-offerings. The second group are said to have lived according to *Maat* while they existed on earth. They in turn are supplied with their own offerings, represented by the bread baskets.

Below, partly preserved on the fragments in Sir John Soane's Museum, are six of an original twelve figures. They tend large ears of barley in the fields of the netherworld, as provision for the blessed dead. The life-giving light cast by Re as he passes touches Osiris and also makes the corn flourish. Beyond is visible one of seven gods who carry sickles to reap the rich harvest.

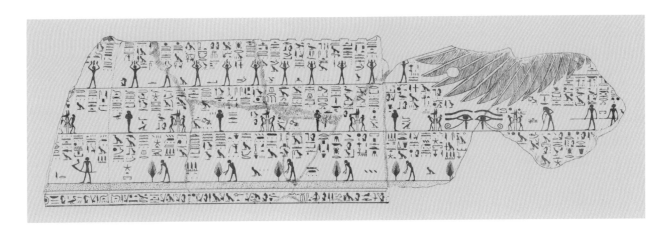

EIGHTH DIVISION
Exterior of lid, left side

The Eighth Hour, too, is incompletely preserved. In the **central register** the solar barque is towed forward, preceded by twelve gods (only seven are visible) who punish the sun-god's enemies and drive them from his presence. In front of them stand two of an original four mummiform figures called 'those with warlike faces'. In the text, the sun-god promises them freedom from their mummy wrappings and uncovering of their faces so that they might see the night sun.

Above are twelve gods, 'those who carry the rope which brings forth "mysteries"'. The 'mysteries' are not clearly defined, but they are represented by human heads, falcon heads and flail-sceptres. These emerge from the rope when Re appears, to conduct him on his way. Beyond are a further twelve gods with another snake-like rope (only partly preserved on the sarcophagus). It is an image of the cyclical nature of time; each hour, represented by a star, emerges from the rope, runs its course and returns inside.

Below right, a figure called 'he with hidden mystery' leans on a staff. This name is a circumlocution for the sun-god, and the 'hidden mystery' is actually

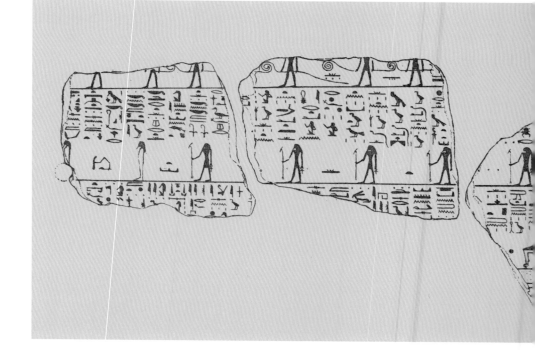

his corpse, concealed in the netherworld. Before him, twelve mummiform figures lie on biers raising up their heads (only six are preserved). These are *akhu*: the blessed dead in the transfigured state. The sun-god calls on them to awaken to life, promising breath for their noses, freedom from their mummy wrappings, offerings and oblations. Their bodies, their *bas* and their shadows – all important elements of the individual – are activated and they are able to enjoy full life. Beyond, totally lost on Seti's sarcophagus, are twelve underworld judge-deities, among whose duties

is the protection of the blessed dead who have newly achieved the status of *akhu*.

The remainder of the *Book of Gates* is carved on the interior of the sarcophagus case, beginning at the left side of the head and proceeding from left to right.

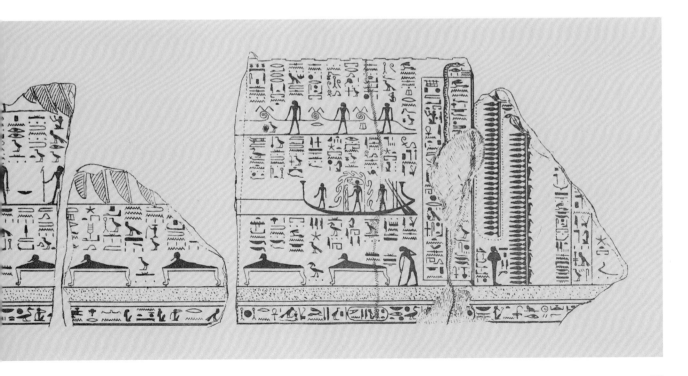

NINTH DIVISION
Interior of case, upper left side
(North side in Museum*)

The **eighth gate**, similar in form to the others, is guarded by a serpent named 'The one with flaming face'. Beyond is seen the sun-god's barque before a schematic representation of a large stretch of water. This is Nun, the primeval ocean, and it is watched over by a figure named as 'he who is in Nun', who is probably the sun-god himself. Sixteen human figures lying in the water in different attitudes represent those who have died by drowning. These blessed dead will be revived by the passage of the sun-god, who promises them air to breathe, freedom of movement, and rejuvenation from the primeval waters. The water is in itself beneficial to the dead; it is a place in which they

are regenerated repeatedly, and once reawakened to life they are able to partake of food offerings to sustain themselves.

Above are twelve divine figures 'who provide bread and distribute [edible] plants' to the *ba*-souls in the 'Island of Fire' (apparently a region of the netherworld). The *ba* was believed to require sustenance, just as was the physical body, and it is the fulfilment of this need that is represented here. Nine birds with human heads and arms represent these *ba*-souls of the dead; each has its provisions – bread in a basket, and vegetables – and they adore the sun-god, who stands before them leaning on a staff.

Below is another depiction of the punishment of the damned. Twelve 'enemies of Osiris', hands bound, proceed towards a giant snake which spews fire at them. At far left, Horus, leaning on a staff, addresses the 'evildoers'. In contrast to the dead in the water above, these individuals will be decapitated and burnt by the fire of the serpent. Their *bas* will be annihilated; they will cease to exist. This is the triumph of Osiris over his enemies, brought about by Horus. In the coils of the serpent stand mummiform 'gods who are upon the "Fiery One"'. They are described as 'children' of Horus (here seven, instead of the four mentioned in other funerary texts) and they assist in bringing the damned to their fiery end.

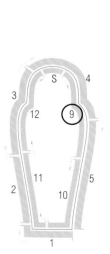

LEFT The eighth gate.

*The compass directions on pp. 60–9 refer to the side of the basement on which the spectator should stand in order to view the section of the decoration described.

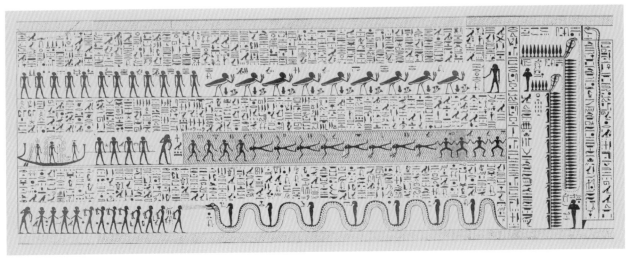

TENTH DIVISION
Interior of case, lower left side and left side of foot end
(North side in Museum)

The solar barque appears again in the **central register**. The text relates how the sun-god's *ba* meets his physical body in the netherworld. By uniting *ba*, body and shadow, the spiritual element of the god takes up residence in his physical form. Thus reconstituted, the god requires protection against his arch-enemy Apophis during the crucial phase when he moves from the netherworld to the sky. Apophis is shown as a large coiled snake at the extreme right-hand end of the register (at the interior of the foot of the sarcophagus), and above him is a crocodile with a snake-headed tail. He is attacked by a long line of figures who use the power of magic to overcome him and protect Re. The largest group of these protectors, comprising male and female figures and apes, hold curved objects which, thanks to a more detailed version of the *Book of Gates* in the tomb of Ramesses VI, can be identified as nets. With the magical force contained in these nets they disable Apophis and render him harmless. Immediately in front of him lies a figure called 'the aged one', who

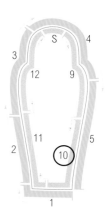

may represent the earth-god Geb. He holds a rope, with which to bind Apophis. This passes behind him and is grasped by three standing figures holding spears, who will attack the hostile snake.

Above, is a double-headed sphinx, with a crowned falcon head and a human head, facing in opposite directions. On the back of the sphinx, stretching out his hands to touch the two crowns, stands 'the two-faced one'. His two heads are those normally associated with the gods Horus and Seth but, despite this iconography, the figure is probably another manifestation of the sun-god. To each side, divine figures haul on a rope which is wound around a sloping stake bearing a crowned human head. The single figure on the left is 'the one who is over the prow-rope'; that on the right is 'the one who is over the stern-rope'. Each is assisted by four gods who wear crowns and uraeus serpents, but who have no heads. Those at the left, wearing the crown of Upper Egypt, are 'Southern Gods', and their counterparts with the crown of Lower Egypt are 'Northern Gods'. The scene and its text alludes to a vessel (not shown) in which the sun-god is travelling and facing in both directions simultaneously.

Next comes an eight-headed snake, provided with human legs and called 'the Walker' (or 'Wanderer)', which is grasped in the middle by a figure who keeps the two halves of the snake apart. The text tells that this dangerous, foul-smelling snake wanders through the whole of the netherworld. It is restrained from threatening the sun-god and the blessed dead by the figure who holds it in the middle. Next to this is a still more complex serpent-being: a snake with eight human heads and sixteen legs, again held in the middle

by a figure named 'Catcher'. Beneath it is another, larger snake with two heads. At the end of the register stand two gods holding stylized nets (like those in the middle register); the text explains that they use magic power on behalf of the sun-god, and they are probably positioned here to overcome the two hostile snakes which they face.

The **lower register** is occupied by a single scene. At the left are four groups of four figures, with the heads of humans, ibises, falcons and rams, named, respectively, 'bas of the West', 'retinue of Thoth', 'retinue of Horus' and 'retinue of Re'. These figures hold the tow-rope of the solar barque, which passes around the human legs of a large double-snake. This is Khepri, the rejuvenated sun, who is more commonly represented as a scarab beetle. In the middle of this is a falcon wearing the double crown, and called 'Horus of the netherworld'. The rope is pulled on the other side by eight figures called 'the Powerful'.

The sun-god is now drawing near to the eastern horizon. These gods have the task of bringing him

there, and they call out: 'To heaven, to heaven, O great one! We place you on your throne by means of the towing-rope which is in our fingers . . .' The depiction of Khepri as a serpent is notable; in the *Amduat* the rejuvenation of the sun-god in the last stages of his journey involves passing through the body of a giant snake.

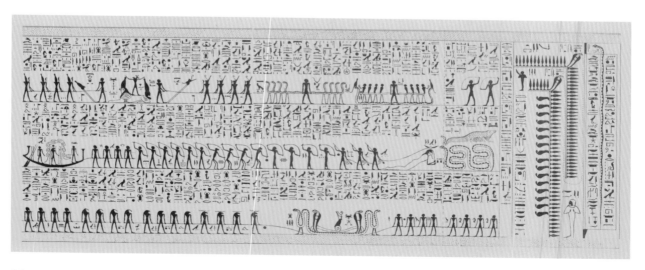

ELEVENTH DIVISION
Interior of case, foot and lower right side
(South side in Museum)

After passing the **tenth gate**, depicted in the middle
of the foot end of the sarcophagus, the solar barque is
pulled along, as before. The text stresses that the sun-
god is now approaching the sky, the goal of his journey,
and the pullers say: 'We are dragging to heaven, we are
dragging to heaven. We follow Re towards heaven.' In
the words which follow, the importance of the god's
face as the dispeller of darkness is emphasized: 'You are
powerful, Re, through your face. You are great, O Re,
when you come to rest in your mysterious face. Re's
face is opened. The two eyes of *Akhty* [the horizon] are
bright when he chases away darkness from the West
. . .' Next comes a figure called 'the hour god' and four
mummiform entities, each with a uraeus serpent on his
head, whose task is to bear the body of the sun-god on
his way.

Now, in a remarkable image, we see the actual
face of the sun-god, depicted frontally, placed in a
barque and protected by a snake. Three gods hold

the tow-rope in one hand and a star in the other; they
probably represent the stars which are to be seen in
the sky before dawn. The text states that they enter
Nut, the sky goddess, whose body was equated with
the heavenly vault. The unusual frontal depiction of
the sun-god's face emphasizes the divine power which
emanates when his glance is turned on the viewer.

Next comes a series of entities who assist Re on his
passage to the eastern horizon. These include a winged
snake named 'the Conductress', and a god called 'the
Flaming One' who holds a torch over a pole, on which
is a bull's head with large horns and, below, a knife.

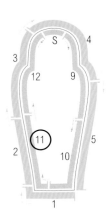

The group probably alludes to the defeat of the sun-god's enemies. Then comes 'the living one', a snake with two human heads, facing Janus-like in opposite directions, and four female figures with arms raised in acclamation, who call to Re to enter the sky. In allusion to the rejuvenation which is supposed to have taken place during his nocturnal journey, they address him as a child who is 'born from the netherworld'. Finally comes a standing figure with two heads (representing Horus and Seth) and two pairs of upraised arms. He is accompanied by six uraeus serpents and stands on two bows, and his role is to 'proclaim Re in the eastern horizon of heaven'.

The **upper register** contains another depiction of the vanquishing of Apophis – this time in detail. There are eight gods grasping cords and knives. Four ('the Fetterers') have human heads; the other four ('the Slaughterers') have each four snakes in the place of heads. Next we see Apophis fettered at the neck, the chains held by the goddess Selkis, who stretches

herself above, but is here shown without arms. Four figures called 'the Enchainers' grasp the other end of the fetters. They stand back-to-back with twelve similar figures also holding a long chain. The other end of this chain passes through the grip of an enormous fist emerging from the earth. This fist belongs to 'the one whose corpse is hidden' – presumably the sun-god. These fetters bind four other snakes, helpers or different manifestations of Apophis, and the group is watched over by Geb, the earth-god, and the four sons of Horus. At the end stands Osiris, 'Foremost of the Westerners'. In the text Re is assured that he can proceed, for Apophis is bound and restrained; Geb and the Sons of Horus are watching over his fetters.

In the **lower register** are twelve gods with oars. They are 'the indestructible gods', i.e. personifications of the circumpolar stars who serve as the crew of the sun-god's barque. The text states: 'It is they who row this great god [Re] after he has taken his seat in the eastern horizon of heaven.' They are here closely

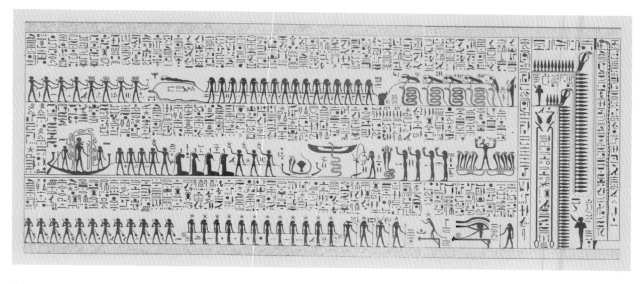

associated with Re's regeneration at dawn; he says
to them: 'Your coming into being is my coming into
being; your birth is my birth.' Next come twelve
hour-goddesses, who tow the barque to the sky. Also
in attendance are gods who assist the sun-god in his
journey: a baboon, the eye of Re himself, and lastly the
doorkeeper of this division of the netherworld.

TWELFTH DIVISION
Interior of case, right side
(South side in Museum)

The **central register** shows the solar barque towed by
four netherworld dwellers, whose speech describes the
transformation undergone by Re in the primeval ocean,
Nun, at morning. The ways to the sky are opened,
and the child sun-god is to be lifted up on the arms of
Nun (as shown in the *Concluding Scene*). Osiris remains
behind in the primeval darkness over which he rules.

Here we see, for the last time, the vanquishing of
Apophis by nine gods who hold sceptres and knives.
Before them is the great serpent himself, bound in
fetters. Next come four apes, each holding a human fist,
who acclaim the sun-god at dawn. The purpose of the
fists is not made clear in the text. Striking the breast
with the fist was a gesture associated with dances of
jubilation, and hence this image may allude to the
celebration of the new dawn, but it may also have an
erotic significance.

Lastly come two goddesses, 'the western one' and
'the one of [the city of] Sais', wearing the crowns

of Upper and Lower Egypt, and a god named 'the
one who belongs to the gate'. Comparison with the
corresponding section in the *Amduat* shows that two
similar goddesses are found there as guardians of the
'Gate of Sais', which is located close to the sun-god's
exit from the netherworld to heaven. The text explains
that these goddesses must turn back when the sun-
god arrives at the gate, but their *bas* go forward in his
following.

The **upper register** commences with four gods
holding sun discs, 'they who carry the sunshine', and
another four holding stars, 'they who carry stars'.
These figures and texts are related to the events which
form the end of the sun-god's journey, when he is raised
from the netherworld and enters the sky. The first four
gods 'unite the netherworld with heaven by means of
this image which is in their hands'; the second four
'make a gesture of praise with their stars' when Re is
received by the arms of Nun.

Next we see eight gods holding sceptres (four with
human heads and four with ram heads). Their role
is to apportion fields and provisions in heaven, just
as was done for the blessed dead in the netherworld.
In this way, continuity is maintained between the
daily and nightly passage of the sun. Then come four
falcon-headed gods, whose role is to set the course of
the solar barque for its journey through the sky. Eight
'protecting star goddesses' are seated on coiled serpents
and holding stars in their hands, while the crocodile-
headed god Sobek-Re holds a sceptre and a snake.
The goddesses rejoice at the sun-god's rising from the
netherworld, and they 'conduct the rowing' of the crew
in the solar barque.

Among the many figures depicted in the **lower register** are deities who perform essential services not only for the sun-god and his retinue as they enter the sky, but also for Osiris. Four figures place crowns on the heads of Re's entourage when they emerge into the heavens. A further four are mourners who 'bewail Osiris after Re has gone out from the hidden region'. At dawn there is both jubilation at Re's entering heaven, and also mourning because Osiris must remain behind in the darkness of the netherworld until the sun-god's

next visit there. In the same manner, the bodies of the blessed dead remain in the netherworld while their *bas* go onward with Re.

Six groups, each composed of four deities, occupy the remaining space. Among these entities are protectors of Re, nurses (appropriate to the sun-god's status as a new-born child), goddesses who ensure the perpetuation of *Maat*, the cosmic order, goddesses who apportion the duration of lifetimes for the damned in the netherworld and for the blessed dead in heaven, mourners for Osiris, and doorkeepers of the netherworld. The final figure, 'the Catlike One', is 'the doorkeeper of the cavern' from which the sun goes forth. The **final gate** of the netherworld is passed, and the sun rises in the sky.

The last gate differs in appearance from the others. Both leaves of the door are depicted, each with a snake guardian; in addition, two serpents representing the goddesses Isis and Nephthys guard the gate. Instead of a group of protective deities, the interior is occupied by two staffs with human heads: Khepri and Atum, the morning and evening forms of the sun-god. The text on the gates records the words of Sia who, in addressing the serpent guardians, says of Re: 'He has come forth from the realm of the dead in order that he may rest in the womb of Nut.' There is also a description of the final closing of the gates of the netherworld: 'Then this door is closed. Then the souls which are in the hidden region lament after this door has slammed.'

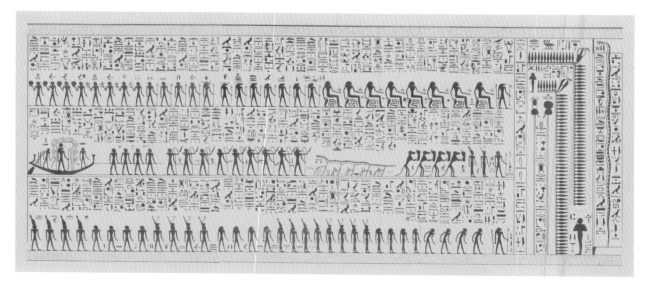

CONCLUDING SCENE
Interior of case, head end

Beyond the gate we see the
sunrise, and the end of Re's
nocturnal journey, represented
in a single large scene which
extends the full height of the
sarcophagus. According to the
mythology of creation, the
sun-god had emerged from the
watery abyss of Nun when the
universe came into existence.
Since each new dawn was
symbolically a new creation,
this scene has a background of
stylized ripples representing
the primeval waters. The god
Nun with arms upraised lifts
up the solar barque from the
depths of the netherworld. A
text between his arms reads:
'These arms come forth from
the water. They lift up this
god.' The barque occupies the
centre of the field. At the prow
stand three 'door[-keepers]'.
Towards the stern are the
deities Geb, Shu, Heqa, Hu
and Sia, the last two manning
the steering oars. In the centre
Isis and Nephthys support the
great scarab beetle which is the
dawn manifestation of the god,
and the text above declares:
'This god takes his seat in

the day-barque.' Above the scarab is a large sun disc which is received into the outstretched hands of the sky-goddess Nut (shown upside down). Nut stands on the head of a strange figure of Osiris, whose body curves into a circle with his feet touching the back of his head; within this circle are the words: 'It is Osiris. He encircles the netherworld.' Osiris, then, is shown here assisting in raising the sun-god to heaven. The whole scene is bounded by a speckled border, through which the sun disc penetrates. This complex image encompasses not only the primeval waters and the sky but also the entire netherworld (encircled by the curved body of Osiris). It is therefore an image of the complete universe in which the cycle of life, death and rebirth was to be endlessly repeated. In keeping with its powerful symbolic worth this scene is deliberately positioned immediately above the head of the dead king's mummy.

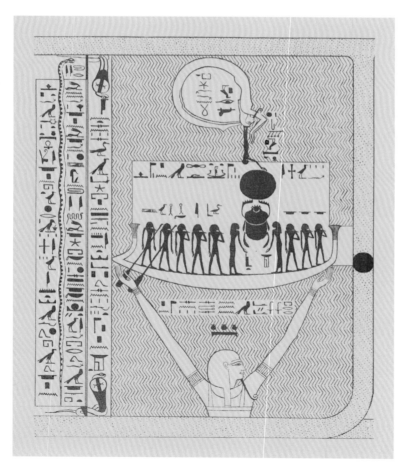

OTHER DECORATION

Although the *Book of Gates* dominates the decoration of the sarcophagus, other figures and texts were also used. The surviving fragments of the lid show that the interior was decorated and extensively inscribed. A solar disc with wings enfolded the head, and at the end of each wing was a figure of the ibis-headed god Thoth, who stands holding a staff on which is the hieroglyphic sign for 'sky'. These figures usually accompany spell 161 of the *Book of the Dead*, and short passages from that text can be identified in the long inscriptions along the edges of the sarcophagus. Jackals representing the gods Anubis or Wepwawet (only the tails of which survive) were carved at each side of the area corresponding to the king's face. Below these was a zone of inscriptions and a large image of a ram-headed falcon whose wings were spread across the breast. In addition to figures of gods, there were further texts from the *Book of the Dead*, including spells 15, 72 and 89 (also repeated on the inside of the case), spells 22 and 23 (which relate to the restoration of the dead person's faculties through the symbolic opening of his mouth) and spell 180, which concerned the uniting of Re and Osiris in the hereafter. The decoration of the lower parts of the body is mostly lost; the remaining portions show that there were two lengthy inscriptions in horizontal lines running from the centre of the lid to the outer edges. A single line of text ran along each outer edge.

The image and texts on the floor of the case, in which the mummy lay, are drawn from sources which have a longer history than the *Book of Gates*. The space

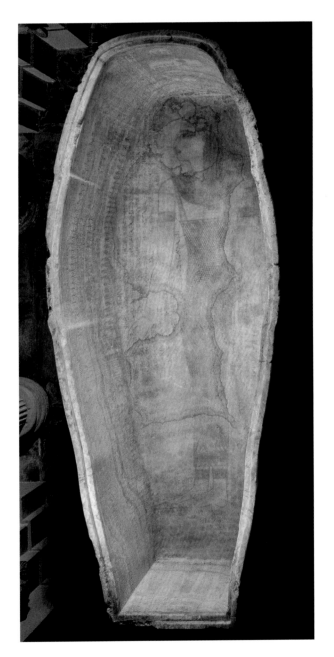

The interior of the sarcophagus, showing the figure of the goddess Nut.

is dominated by a large figure of the goddess Nut. She is depicted standing, wearing a fillet with streamers, a collar and a close-fitting dress which has a pattern of feathers. Armlets, bracelets and anklets complete her costume, and the hieroglyphic signs which spell her name are written above her head. The goddess, while personifying the sky, was also closely identified with the coffin or sarcophagus. When the mummy was placed inside it the deceased symbolically entered the womb of Nut, at which point he was in a state of potential rebirth, ready to enter upon new life. Around the figure are inscribed hieroglyphic texts in horizontal and vertical lines. These begin with speeches of the dead king and of Geb and Nut, the deities who represented earth and sky, which assure the king protection and eternal life. The texts continue with selected spells from the *Book of the Dead*. The first of these is spell 72, which enabled the deceased to leave the tomb by day and return to it again, and to receive offerings in the realm of Osiris. This is followed by spell 89, a highly important text which makes possible the uniting of the spiritual element known as the *ba* with the corpse. This conjunction of physical and non-physical aspects of the dead person was regarded as an essential prerequisite for rebirth and is a recurring theme in the *Book of Gates*.

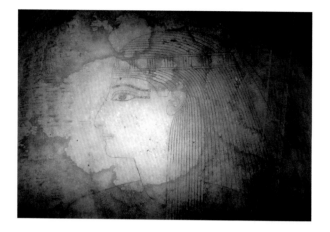

RIGHT Details of the figure of Nut.

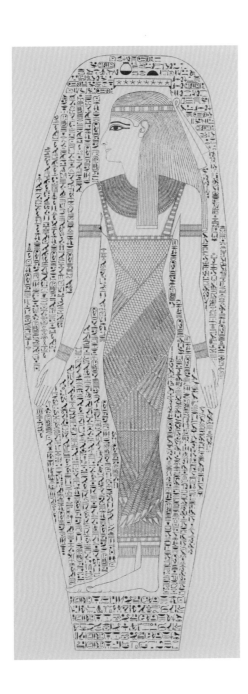

Conclusion

T HE FASCINATION WHICH the sarcophagus held for Soane has proved to be an enduring one, and there is a striking symmetry in the story of its travels. Having been designed as the focal point in the burial chamber of the most sumptuously decorated of all Egyptian royal tombs, it was installed 3,000 years later in Lincoln's Inn Fields as the centrepiece of another crypt, very different in purpose yet conceived with just such a monument in mind. The centre of Soane's sepulchral basement had nonetheless remained vacant since its construction, as though awaiting the sarcophagus' arrival. But while the sarcophagus relates intimately to its present surroundings, it is itself of unique historical importance, as an unequalled testimony to the religious thought and artistic achievements of ancient Egypt in the time of one of its greatest rulers.

NOTES

1 There is some evidence that the entrance to the tomb had been discovered earlier by a native of the village of Qurna, on the west bank of the Nile at Luxor. The credit for the full exploration and documentation of the tomb, and the retrieval of the sarcophagus, however, belongs to Belzoni: B. Gessler-Löhr 2013

2 G.B. Belzoni, *Narrative of the Operations and Recent Discoveries within the Pyramids, Temples, Tombs, and Excavations, in Egypt and Nubia*, 3rd edition (London, 1822), I, 365–6. Belzoni also published a plan and section of the tomb in *Plates illustrative of the Researches and Operations of G. Belzoni in Egypt and Nubia* (London, 1820–22), pl.40. A further account of the tomb was published to accompany the exhibition at the Egyptian Hall, Piccadilly: G.B. Belzoni, *Description of the Egyptian Tomb discovered by G. Belzoni* (London, 1821)

3 The fragments of the lid were initially left behind in Samuel Briggs' warehouse 'packed up in a mat' and were despatched to the British Museum from Cairo some time after 10 May 1822. See J. J. Halls, *The Life and Correspondence of Henry Salt* (London, 1834), II, 336–7

4 Agreement between Salt and Belzoni, 20 April 1818, cited in J. J. Halls, *The Life and Correspondence of Henry Salt* (London, 1834), II, 28–9

5 Belzoni to Salt, 24 Jan. 1822: J. J. Halls, *The Life and Correspondence of Henry Salt* (London, 1834), II, 335

6 The *New Monthly Magazine and Literary Journal* published a ninety-line 'Address to the Alabaster Sarcophagus lately deposited in the British Museum'. It is almost anonymous, the author given only as 'H', and is a classic example of ponderous Georgian verse

7 J.G. Children, 'On the Nature of the Pigment in the Hieroglyphics on the Sarcophagus, from the Tomb of Psammis', *Annals of Philosophy*, N.S. vol II, 1821, 389–390

8 Resolution of the Trustees of the British Museum, cited in Taylor Combe to Bingham Richards, 20 Sept. 1822: See J. J. Halls, *The Life and Correspondence of Henry Salt* (London, 1834), II, 340

9 Yorke to Bingham Richards, 30 Jan 1824, cited in Halls, II, 369. Charles Philip Yorke (1764–1834), a politician, was a Fellow of the Royal Society. His elder half-brother, Philip Yorke, third earl of Hardwicke (1757–1834) met Soane in Italy on the Grand Tour and later commissioned him to make additions to Wimpole Hall, Cambridgeshire. He was also FRS and FSA and a Trustee of the British Museum. The *Morning Post* of 19 April 1824 praised Soane's patriotism in saving the sarcophagus from leaving the country and reported rumours that French and Bavarian agents had been sent to London in the hope of securing it for their governments

10 Soane's Library includes copies of Belzoni's 1820 *Narrative* and *Plates illustrative of the researches and operations of G. Belzoni in Egypt and Nubia*. He also purchased Belzoni's *Six new plates illustrative of the researches and operations of G. Belzoni in Egypt and Nubia*, published in 1822, and his *Voyages en Égypte et en Nubie, contenant le réit des recherches et découvertes archéologiques faites dans les pyramides, temples, ruines et tombes de ce pays. Suivis d'un voyage sur la cote de la Mer Rouge. . .*, 1821

11 SM Archive Priv. Corr. II.T.13.1. Soane had let out his own first home in Lincoln's Inn Fields, which he built in 1792–94 since moving next door to No. 13 in 1813

12 Ledger E under payments from Soane's account with Grote, Prescott for 1824 lists 'Mr. S [for] sarcophagus. April 15th [paid] Salte £2,000'. Soane's Office Day Book April 15 1824 records the payment 'Mr Soane / Paid Salte Esq're / for the Belzoni sarcaophgus / (Grote & Co.) £2000'

13 The fragments of the lid were presumably delivered on the same day. Two days later on 14 May, Soane's Notebook records a cryptic conversation with Mr. and Mrs Tyndale about whether or not the 'top of the sarcophagus' belonged to Soane

14 The *Morning Post* 15 May 1824

15 Four large brackets, bolted through the four corner columns of the 'Dome area' of Soane's Museum, the double-height space through which the sarcophagus had

to be lowered, probably relate to the installation and may have supported horizontal beams to which ropes and pulleys could have been attached

16 Eric George, *The Life and Death of Benjamin Robert Haydon* (1948), 139; Helen Dorey, 'Sir John Soane's Acquisition of the Sarcophagus of Seti I', *Georgian Group Journal* (1991), 33

17 There was obviously some discussion about how it should be installed. A letter dated 27 August 1824 from Walter Payne (clerk of works), at the Bank of England, to John Soane (presumably out of town at the time) reporting on progress with projects includes the paragraph: *'The Coffin will look better from above when raised up and I do not see a step on each side will be in the way.'* SM Archive 8/88/77. In an engraving for Soane's *Public and Private Buildings*, 1828, the sarcophagus is shown supported by two pairs of naturalistic lion's feet

18 The canopic chest fragment is published in: Aidan Dodson, *The Canopic Equipment of the Kings of Egypt* (London and New York, 1994), 68–9, 126, 172–3, pl. XXIXb (no. 36)

19 In a letter from Gandy to John Soane, dated 12 Nov 1825, later than the watercolours, one paragraph may hint at these reconstructions and certainly shows in what detail the sarcophagus was studied. Gandy writes: *'From the fragments it appears the cover of the Sarcophagus was coved external and interior 15 inches high supporting a flat roof the head end rising a little higher than the other parts, and from thence it sloped to the foot where it finished square, coved like many of the shrine roofs seen amongst the pictures on the sarcophagus itself. The head inside formed a kind of half dome on which is figured something like a winged Globe.'* (SM Archive Priv. Corr. III.G.1.55)

20 The fragments of the lid remain in these late 19th-century cases which are in store, available to researchers on request. It is hoped that a new scholarly analysis of the pieces will be carried out in the next few years

21 The name of the king did not become recognized as Seti (or 'Sety') until the late 19th century. Early writers rendered the name as 'Psammis' or 'Psammuthis', while Bonomi and Sharpe published the sarcophagus in 1864 as that of 'Oimenepthah', a translation which encompassed the phrase 'Mer-en-Ptah' ('Beloved of the god Ptah'), which was regularly added to the king's birth-name, Seti, in inscriptions

22 The evidence for the chronology of the reign is summarized in Hornung, Krauss and Warburton 2006, 210–11. If, as has been suggested, the reading of 'Year 11' on an inscription from Gebel Barkal is to be emended to 'Year 3', then Seti's highest recorded regnal date would be Year 9

23 Royal mummies from the Deir el-Bahri cache remain on display in the Egyptian Museum, Cairo

24 Sir John Soane's Museum: Curatorial papers. The Trustees Minutes reveal that this matter was first raised in a letter from Mr Tompkins to James Wild (Curator) 'about two years ago'. The content of this letter was reported to the Trustees of the Soane Museum on 20 July 1891 (Minute Book 3, pp.44–46), so Mr Tompkins had written in about 1889. Mr Hobson was made Curator *pro tem* between the death of George Bailey and the appointment of Joseph Bonomi. Later Trustees Minutes reveal that three further letters on the subject were received by the next Curator, Wyatt Papworth, dated 23 June, 3 July and 18 July 1893

25 G. Verri and J.C. Ambers, 'Examination of pigment traces and repairs on the sarcophagus of Seti I, Sir John Soane's Museum, London' (unpublished analytical report, AR2008/63, The British Museum, London, 22 October 2008)

26 The magical power which was believed to reside within the texts and images needed to be carefully controlled to avoid harming the dead, as the inscriptions on the sarcophagus show. The name of Seti I incorporated a hieroglyphic sign representing the god Seth, the murderer of Osiris, and to eliminate any negative forces that this image might activate in the sarcophagus, a small figure of Osiris was substituted for that of Seth wherever the name occurred

27 A fragment of the lid of a calcite royal sarcophagus in the British Museum (EA 29948) preserves part of the seventh division of the *Book of Gates*. On account of the close similarity of its design, it has been suggested that this piece may have formed part of the sarcophagus lid of Seti I, but no royal name appears in the surviving inscriptions and, as other pharaohs (such as Ramesses II and Merenptah) possessed similar calcite sarcophagi, a firm attribution to a specific ruler cannot be made

BIBLIOGRAPHY

Belzoni, Giovanni B., *Narrative of the Operations and Recent Discoveries within the pyramids, temples, tombs, and excavations in Egypt and Nubia*, 3rd ed., (London, 1822)

Bonomi, Joseph and Sharpe, Samuel, *The Alabaster Sarcophagus of Oimenepthah I., King of Egypt, now in Sir John Soane's Museum, Lincoln's Inn Fields* (London, 1864)

Brand, Peter J., 'The "Lost" Obelisks and Colossi of Seti I', *Journal of the American Research Center in Egypt* 34 (1997), 101–114

Brand, Peter J, *The Monuments of Seti I. Epigraphic, Historical and Art Historical analysis* (Leiden, Boston, Köln, 2000)

Budge, E.A. Wallis, *Sir John Soane's Museum. An Account of the Sarcophagus of Seti I. King of Egypt, B. C. 1370* (London, 1908)

Calverley, Amice M. and Broome, Myrtle F., *The Temple of King Sethos I at Abydos*, 4 vols (London and Chicago, 1933–58)

Dorey, Helen, 'Sir John Soane's acquisition of the sarcophagus of Seti I', *Georgian Group Journal* (1991), 26–35

Gessler-Löhr, Beatrix, 'Who discovered "Belzoni's Tomb"? A glimpse behind the scenes of early exploration and the antiquities trade' in M. Betro and G. Miniaci, *Talking along the Nile. Ippolito Rosellini, travellers and scholars of the 19th century in Egypt* (Pisa, 2013), 101–123

Halls, J.J., *The Life and Correspondence of Henry Salt, Esq. FRS &c.*, 2 vols (London, 1834)

Hornung, Erik, *Das Buch von den Pforten des Jenseits*, I–II. Aegyptiaca Helvetica 7–8 (Geneva, 1979–80)

Hornung, Erik, *The Valley of the Kings*, translated by David Warburton (New York, 1990)

Hornung, Erik, *The Tomb of Pharaoh Seti I. Das Grab Sethos' I* (Zürich and Munich, 1991)

Hornung, Erik, *The Ancient Egyptian Books of the Afterlife*, translated by David Lorton (Ithaca and London, 1999)

Hornung, Erik and Abt, Theodor, *The Egyptian Book of Gates* (Zurich, 2014)

Hornung, E., Krauss, R. and Warburton, D. A. (eds), *Ancient Egyptian Chronology* (Leiden and Boston, 2006)

Jenni, Hanna, 'Totenbuch- und andere Sprüche auf dem Deckel des Sarkophages Sethos' I', *Göttinger Miszellen* 236 (2013), 31–41

Kitchen, K. A., *Pharaoh Triumphant. The Life and Times of Ramesses II, King of Egypt* (Warminster, 1982)

Kitchen, K. A., *Ramesside Inscriptions Translated and Annotated: Translations I. Ramesses I, Sethos I and Contemporaries* (Oxford, 1993)

Manley, Deborah and Ree, Peta, *Henry Salt. Artist, Traveller, Diplomat, Egyptologist* (London, 2001)

Masquelier-Loorius, Julie, *Séthi Ier et le début de la XIXe dynastie* (Paris, 2013)

Mayes, Stanley, *The Great Belzoni* (London, 1959)

Maystre, Charles and Piankoff, Alexandre, *Le Livre des Portes. Texte*, I–III (Cairo, 1939–1962)

Murnane, William J. *The Road to Kadesh. A Historical Interpretation of the Battle Reliefs of King Seti I at Karnak*, 2nd ed., revised (Chicago, 1990)

Osing, Jürgen, *Der Tempel Sethos' I in Gurna. Die Reliefs und Inschriften*. Band I (Mainz am Rhein, 1977)

Reeves, C. Nicholas, *Valley of the Kings. The decline of a royal necropolis* (London and New York, 1990)

Reeves, N. and Wilkinson, R. H., *The Complete Valley of the Kings. Tombs and Treasures of Egypt's Greatest Pharaohs* (London, 1996)

Solia, Victoria, 'A group of royal sculptures from Abydos', *Journal of the American Research Center in Egypt* 29 (1992), 107–122

Spalinger, Anthony J., 'The Northern Wars of Seti I: an Integrative Study', *Journal of the American Research Center in Egypt* 16 (1979), 29–46

University of Chicago, Oriental Institute, *The Battle Reliefs of King Seti I*. Reliefs and Inscriptions at Karnak 4 (Chicago, 1985)

This is an updated and expanded version of an article that first appeared in *The Georgian Group Journal* 1991.

Sir John Soane's reception of the sarcophagus of Seti I

by Helen Dorey

IN OCTOBER 1817 GIOVANNI BELZONI, Italian strong-man turned Egyptologist, entered the tomb of pharaoh Seti I in the Valley of the Kings in Egypt. Within the tomb, in a chamber he christened the 'Hall of Pillars', he found 'a sarcophagus of the finest oriental alabaster, 9'5" long and 3'7" wide . . . [and] transparent when a light is placed in the inside'.[1] This sarcophagus today rests in the 'Sepulchral Chamber' at the heart of the basement of Sir John Soane's Museum in Lincoln's Inn Fields.

When Belzoni made his discovery he was working under the patronage of the British Consul-General in Egypt, Henry Salt (1780–1827), and it was Salt who had the Sarcophagus conveyed to England in 1821 on the frigate HMS *Diana*.[2] On arrival it was deposited in the British Museum on 28 September 1821, this arrangement in theory pending its purchase by the Museum's Trustees.[3]

It is clear that Soane was deeply interested in the sarcophagus from the outset. He kept newspaper cuttings relating to its discovery and purchased a copy of Belzoni's 1820 *Narrative of the Operations and Recent Discoveries within the Pyramids, Temples, Tombs, and Excavations in Egypt and Nubia*.[4] In the same year he purchased a set of the *Plates Illustrative of the Researches and Operations of G. Belzoni in Egypt and Nubia* which included several views of the sarcophagus. Soane's

Notebook [his diary] records that on February 12, 1822 he visited the British Museum at 1pm and notes that he purchased a Belzoni publication for a friend.[5] He presumably made this visit in order to see the recently arrived sarcophagus – probably for the first time.

On June 8 the *Notebook* records that he was 'At Mr Belzoni's Exhibition'. This exhibition, held at the Egyptian Hall, Piccadilly, comprised a full-size model of two chambers in the tomb of Seti I, reconstructed using 'casts in plaster of Paris, from wax impressions [made] on the spot', and many objects from the tomb.[6] Soane purchased a copy of the *Description of the Egyptian Tomb* which accompanied the exhibition, price 1 shilling.[7] This provided a much more vivid and sensational account of Belzoni's Egyptian discoveries than the earlier *Narrative*, dwelling long on the lack of air in the tombs, the piles of decaying mummies and suffocating dust encountered and the various emotions experienced.

Despite Belzoni's highly popular accounts of his discoveries and the public interest and excitement generated by them and by his exhibition, the British Museum Trustees baulked at Salt's asking price of £2,000 for the sarcophagus. Negotiations were prolonged and it was not until February 13, 1824 that Soane approached his neighbour, George Booth Tyndale, a Trustee of the British Museum, asking

Joseph Michael Gandy, view of
the Dome Area by night, 1811.
This watercolour, although drawn
fourteen years before Soane's
receptions for the arrival of
the sarcophagus, shows how
the Museum looked at night,
dramatically lit from a light
source in the basement.

if he could obtain for him the 'first refusal' of the sarcophagus in the event of the British Museum not purchasing it.[8] Negotiations then continued throughout March between Tyndale, acting as Soane's agent, and Bingham Richards, Henry Salt's agent. On April 1 Soane instructed Tyndale that if the British Museum Trustees had not decided by the end of the month he would be compelled to decline any further thought of purchasing the sarcophagus. On April 12 Tyndale reported that the British Museum had finally resolved not to purchase and on the 13th Bingham Richards wrote to Soane direct, accepting his offer of £2,000 and enclosing the order for the transfer and delivery of the sarcophagus to Soane.[9] Belzoni himself did not receive a penny from the sale of the sarcophagus because his agreement with Salt was that he would receive half of any proceeds over and above the first £2,000.

Soane's purchase was reported enthusiastically in the newspapers, cuttings from which he carefully preserved in a series of large scrapbooks.[10] On April 22 the *Morning Post* reported, 'we believe that there is no country in Europe which would not be proud of possessing such a rarity and that the Emperor of Russia, in particular, would rejoice to obtain it, if it were possible to purchase it from the liberal and patriotic individual who is now its proprietor.' Other papers referred additionally, with a certain amount of glee, to the thwarting of French and Bavarian agents in London who had hoped to obtain the sarcophagus for their countries.

On May 12 Soane's *Notebook* records, 'Sarcophagus brought this day.' *The Sun* on May 14 noted, 'On account of its magnitude it was necessary to make a wide opening in the back of [Mr. Soane's] house.' The sarcophagus was lowered down through the dome from the ground floor probably using ropes attached to metal cramps (which can still be seen in

the backs of the four dome piers) and placed in its present position. The reception of the sarcophagus prompted Soane to re-work the rest of the basement of his Museum, creating a new 'Ante-Room to the Belzoni Sarcophagus' from what had previously been the Housekeeper's Room (reducing the extent of his domestic offices quite considerably by doing so). Its creation, along with that of the Catacombs, in 1824 deliberately created a new route to the heart of the basement focused on the sarcophagus.

The acquisition of the sarcophagus was Soane's greatest coup as a collector. It eclipsed all his other purchases and cost more than any of them. As soon as he saw it he must have known that it would make an ideal centrepiece for his Museum. He referred to his own 'melancholy and brooding' temperament and seems to have revelled in the morbid and funereal. From its inception he had envisaged a mausoleum and catacombs in the basement of his Museum and the acquisition of the sarcophagus provided the ideal focus for this area. He was fascinated by its antiquity and the 'human industry and perseverance'[11] involved in its creation as well as by the mystery of the indecipherable hieroglyphics and unknown occupant. It never ceased to be a focus for his attention and ten years after its acquisition, in 1834–35, he sacrificed his large wine cellar, located next to it at the east end of the basement, to create an 'Egyptian crypt' filled with funerary monuments of his own day.

John Britton's description of Soane's Museum in *The Union of Architecture, Sculpture and Painting,* 1827, must reflect Soane's own views and shows that the sarcophagus appealed for its sublime and romantic qualities. Britton writes 'how frivolous and insipid a gew-gaw is the largest diamond in the world, in comparison. It contains no meaning, exacts no emotion but pecuniary value; creates no deep interest; nor does it awaken any latent sentiment of mind.' Just a few days before the sarcophagus was installed at Lincoln's Inn Fields news of Belzoni's death in Africa reached London. Soane always referred to his greatest treasure as 'the Belzoni sarcophagus' and obviously regarded it as a sort of shrine to its discoverer.[12]

Immediately after Belzoni's death his widow, Sarah, issued an engraving of the explorer, showing him surrounded by the principal antiquities he had discovered – Soane naturally purchased a copy (see p. 8). She also began planning a new exhibition of the Egyptian tomb to be held at 28 Leicester Square 'for the support of Mr. Belzoni's aged mother and numerous relatives at Padua'.[13] *The Morning Chronicle* for 11 December 1824 announced that the exhibition might include the sarcophagus itself since one of the conditions of the sale to John Soane was that it could be repurchased by Belzoni or his heirs. On 9 February 1825, Soane received a letter from the Rev. G.A. Browne of Trinity College, Cambridge, writing on behalf of Mrs Belzoni, asking whether, if she could raise the sum paid by Soane, the sarcophagus would be given up to her in time for its being placed in her exhibition of the tomb. The letter explains that Mrs Belzoni has been told by W. Bankes that the Trustees of the British Museum handed the sarcophagus over to Soane with the full understanding that he would relinquish it to Mr or Mrs Belzoni for the price given for it to Bingham Richards. Soane immediately wrote back saying that no such understanding existed and adding that he could not conceive from what source the information was derived.[14] This correspondence was published in *The Sun* on March 9 by 'J.B.' (presumably John Britton) with a paragraph repudiating Mrs Belzoni's claim. Soane was obviously extremely anxious to avoid any bad publicity.

It seems to have been this correspondence and a desire to help Mrs Belzoni to make her exhibition a success that prompted Soane to throw open his house on 23, 26 and 30 March 1825 for three receptions in honour of the sarcophagus. *The Literary Gazette* reported that Soane's 'avowed object was to interest [his guests] in the Exhibition of Egyptian Antiquities, which the widow of the unfortunate Belzoni is about to produce in Leicester Square'. In addition, however, the three evenings, were also, of course, opportunities for Soane to create a great spectacle.

The preparations were meticulous and all the bills are carefully preserved in the Soane Archive.[15] John Britton was closely involved in the organisation, ordering some of the invitations and paying for various items himself and being reimbursed by Soane later. Invitation cards were ordered from Thomas Greswick, 16 Skinner Street, Snowhill, tinted and buff, large and small. Examples of both colours are pasted into Soane's press-cuttings volume and the copper plate used in the engraving (by Benjamin Davies in Compton Street) also survives in the Museum. On March 22, 23, 24, 26 and 28, Soane's pupils were engaged in arranging drawings and in writing invitation cards.[16] More

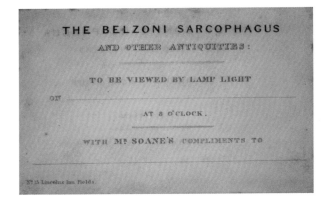

Invitation to view the sarcophagus by lamplight, March 1825.

than 890 recipients were invited, with Mr Soane's compliments, to view 'The Belzoni Sarcophagus and other antiquities . . . by lamp light', at 8 o'clock on one of the three evenings. Staff were employed for all three nights: two waiters at 7s each, Anne Essell and Ann Jones at 5s each and a 'Beadle and Gardner' at 10s each. Three nights-worth of ale and porter at £1 14s 6d was purchased, presumably for the servants, along with a quantity of brandy.

The main beverages served to guests were tea and coffee. '5lb mixt tea. ½lb Hyson Tea' and '½lb of Souchong Tea' was purchased from James Parlett and '½lb Turkey Coffee' from Turnford & Rice, Coffee dealers of 6 Skinner Street, Snowhill. The total amount of loaf and beat [sic] sugar purchased for the three nights was 31lb.

Guests were also offered a selection of cakes purchased from Robinson and Todd, Confectioners, of 79 Fleet Street – different quantities of each on each night. For example, on 26th they consumed '4 pound cakes, 1 doz sweet rusks, 1 doz Ita[sic =?Italian] biscuits, 2 doz water cakes and 1 doz tea cakes'.

However, the most elaborate planning was that of the lighting in the Museum for the three evenings. As well as purchasing 8lb 'Palace wax lights' and 3lb wax candles from Davies' Candle, Soap and Oil Warehouse at 162 Fleet Street, Soane engaged outside contractors to supply additional lighting. John Patrick of 94 Newgate Street, was paid £24 15s, 'To illuminat'g the outside of Mr Soane's House with 182 Glass Bucket Lamps and 74 Glass Barrel Lamps, 3 nights . . .@ £8 5s pr. nt'. William Collins, manufacturer of stained glass and dealer in lighting appliances, was engaged to provide (on hire) 108 lamps, chandeliers and candelabra to be placed or suspended around the ground-floor rooms and in the basement. It seems that the guests were not expected to go upstairs to the drawing rooms at all.

Soane himself must have supervised the placing of all the lamps and Collins' bill reflects very precise requirements detailing which lamps were placed in which apartments. Soane refers in his 1830 *Description* to 'those fanciful effects that constitute the poetry of Architecture'[17] created in his house by his manipulation of space and use of light. Collins' bill enables us to see how he lit the ground floor and basement at night to exploit to the full all the contrasts of light with gloom around the house and to create the maximum romantic atmosphere in which to appreciate the sarcophagus.

The entrance hall was well lit with a lantern with a two-light burner and two 'French lamps' with pedestals. The Library was allocated two large four-light candelabra, two two-light antique lamps, two single-light 'rich pedestal lamps' and two single-light bronze lamps. Additionally, three lamps were placed outside the Dining Room window in the Monument Court, which would have enabled guests to see the sculpture arranged around the parapets of the roof above and also to view the *Pasticcio* (a column of architectural fragments) in the centre of the courtyard.[18]

In the Breakfast Room the lighting was modest, just two 'rich five-light candelabra'. This presumably enabled the more than 100 mirrors in the room to provide most of the light by reflection.

A chandelier and four lamps were placed in Soane's 'Old Gallery'. This was his first Picture Room which was on the site of the present New Picture Room (built in 1889; this space re-opened after refurbishment in autumn 2016 renamed again as The Foyle Space). In addition for this room Collins hired out to Soane 'a large looking-glass' – this must have wonderfully increased the fanciful effects around the adjacent Dome Area by reflection. In the Dome itself four three-light lamps were suspended and there were also

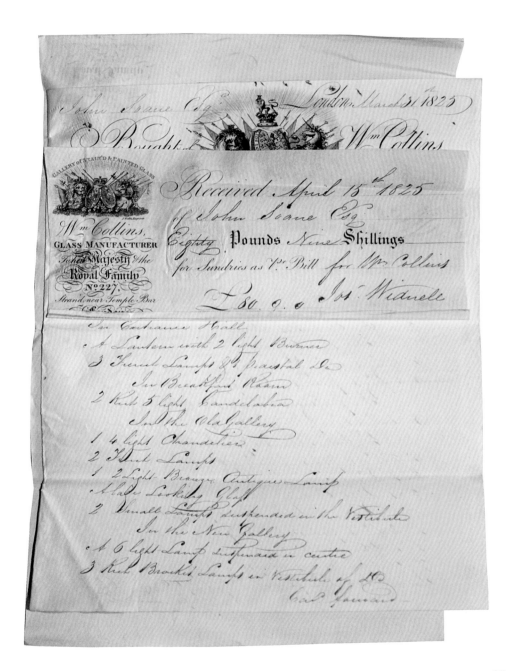

The first page of William Collins' bill for lighting the Museum for the receptions on 23, 26 and 30 March, 1825.

LEFT Joseph Michael Gandy, *Public and Private Buildings Executed by John Soane between 1780 and 1815*, watercolour, 1818, detail to show the reflector, presumably mirrored on the other side, from which lamplight shines out illuminating the models around it.

OPPOSITE The sarcophagus with its cover removed showing the effect in daylight when it is lit by candles from within.

four single-light French lamps (presumably around the balustrades) and two one-light bracket lamps – perhaps fixed to two of the piers. The hanging lamps would have illuminated the sarcophagus from above very effectively as well as casting a good light on to the various antiquities displayed around the Dome itself. Four large hooks survive, fixed to the inner rim of the Dome, which must have been for hanging these lamps.

Soane's 'New Gallery', the present Picture Room, was lit by one six-light lamp suspended in the centre.[19] This room had recently been completed and many of the guests must have been seeing it for the first time and of course viewing Soane's outstanding Canaletto and Hogarth paintings on display there.

As for the basement, Collins' bill shows that lighting was much less widespread than on the ground floor – in order to heighten the romantic and funereal effect. The Monk's Parlour, another recently completed room[20], was given four two-light pedestal lamps, two single-light French lamps and two single-light bronze lamps. These must have been placed at waist height on the various tables and would have allowed the effect of the stained glass window reflected in the mirrors to be fully appreciated. The basement passages and the catacombs do not seem to have been lit at all but around the sarcophagus itself were placed one two-light pedestal lamp, one single-light pedestal lamp with reflector and seven 'jappanned lamps'. The pedestal lamp with reflector may have been similar to the one, with Soane's coat-of-arms on it, shown in an earlier imaginary view of Soane's built works (illustrated left).

The *New Times* on March 24 commented that the sarcophagus 'seemed to be of a red colour, owing to the red light of the lamps by which it was illuminated'. This is almost certainly an inaccurate description as it would not have been necessary for the lamps themselves to produce a red light for the sarcophagus to glow red.

The effect is produced by placing a light adjacent to the stone without the need for any coloured filter. It seems likely that candles were placed inside the sarcophagus (rather safer than lamps full of oil). A small piece of corroborative evidence that visitors were shown the sarcophagus in this way later in the 19th century is provided by Dr Gustav Waagen in a short reivew of the Museum published in 1855 when he says of the coffin: 'The stone is so transparent, that, when a candle is put into the sarcophagus, it appears of a beautiful red.'[21]

The total cost of Collins' lighting was £80 9s and the lamps consumed '36 Gallons of best oil'.

All three evening parties were widely reported in the newspapers which noted the presence of 'distinguished fashionables and literary characters', 'persons versed in antiquarian lore', MPs and Royal Academicians as well as 'private friends and elegant females'. The company seems to have remained 'on the spot till a late hour' each night. Mr Allen (the Master of Dulwich College) writing to thank Soane for the 'very great treat' he had experienced, mentions that he did not arrive until after 11 o'clock. Allen does not mention the sarcophagus at all in his letter but says that Soane's antiquities were 'rendered infinitely more attractive by the Beautiful Women who adorn'd the several apartments'.[22] Mrs Belzoni attended the first reception and *The Literary Gazette*, under the heading 'Sketches of Society, Sights of London', reported that she 'received every attention from the guests of her kind patron'. Among the guests present on the 30th, the last reception, listed in *The Sun* on the 31st, were 'Mr. Peel'[23] and Don Bernardino Rividavia[24], 'one of the Founders of the Republic of Bueno Ayres, a gentleman conspicuous for integrity and learning'.

The grandest of the three occasions, however, seems to have been Saturday, March 26. *The Sun* reported, 'Among the splendid circle of visitors on this occasion we noticed, The Duke of Susex, Lord and Lady Liverpool, the Chancellor of the Exchequer . . . Lord Gifford, Lady Ellenborough . . . Lord and Lady Caledon, Sir Abraham Hume, Sir Charles Long, the Bishop of London . . . Sir Thomas Lawrence, Sir William Beechey . . . Mr. Colridge [sic] the poet . . . and many other persons of well-known taste.' Soane

obviously took great care to ensure in particular that his royal guest was well looked after. Unfortunately, on the morning of the 26th, he received a letter from James Curtin (an assistant of Belzoni's who was also responsible for the erecting of the model of the Egyptian tomb for Mrs Belzoni's Exhibition at Leicester Square), regretting that owing to a sprained ankle he would not be able to 'attend . . . for the purpose of giving some explanation to His Royal Highness the Duke of Sussex concerning the Belzoni Sarcophagus'.[25] Despite this setback Soane must have been extremely gratified by the royal presence, particularly as the Duke had belonged to the same masonic lodge as Belzoni and had been referred to by the explorer as 'my patron and friend'.[26]

A marvellous description survives by Benjamin Robert Haydon, the diarist, writing to Mary Russell Mitford, of the Saturday reception. 'The first person I met . . . was Coleridge . . . [then] I was pushed against Turner, the landscape painter[27], with this red face and white waistcoat, and . . . was carried off my legs and irretrievably bustled to where the sarcophagus lay. Soane's house is a perfect Cretan labyrinth: curious narrow staircases, landing places, balconies, spring doors, and little rooms filled with fragments to the very ceiling. It was the finest fun imaginable to see the people come in to the library after wandering about below, amidst tombs and capitals, and shafts and noiseless heads, with a sort of expression of delighted relief at finding themselves again among the living, and with coffee and cake! Fancy delicate ladies of fashion dipping their pretty heads into an old mouldy, fusty, hieroglphicked coffin, blessing their stars at its age, wondering whom it contained and whispering that it was mentioned in Pliny. You can imagine the associations connected with such contrasts. Just as I was beginning to meditate, the Duke of Sussex, with

LEFT The sarcophagus lit by candles from within, the effect at night in the unlit basement.

89

a star on his breast and an asthma inside it, came squeezing and wheezing along the narrow passage, driving all the women before him like a Blue-Beard, and putting his royal head into the coffin, added his wonder to the wonder of the rest. Upstairs stood Soane, spare, thin, caustic, and starched, "mocking the thing he laughed at" as he smiled approbation for the praises bestowed on his magnificent house.' [28]

For Soane these three receptions were a triumph. So much did they fulfil his romantic vision of the sarcophagus and his Museum that 10 years later he included a poetical account of the sarcophagus by lamp light, written by the novelist Barbara Hofland, in his 1835 *Description* of his house. It is long but loses much if cut:

'If, in the hour of midday splendour, the sarcophagus appears only a superb and suitable finish to the works of art by which it is surrounded, and more calculated to complete the impression conveyed by the whole, than to claim exclusive and individual preference; it should be viewed by lamplight also. Seen by this medium every surrounding object . . . becomes subservient to the sarcophagus . . . all . . . are but accessories to its dignity and grandeur; a mingled sense of awe, admiration, and delight pervades our faculties and is even oppressive in its intensity, yet endearing in its associations; for sweet and tender memories unite us to the grave. Deep masses of shadow, faint gleams that rise like *ignes fatui* from the adjoining crypt, lights that shine like lustrous halos round marble heads, others more vague and indistinct, yet beautiful in their revealings, present appearances beheld as in a dream of the poet's Elysium; and without enlarging the objects, the scene itself, under this artificial illumination, appears considerably expanded. By degrees this space becomes peopled – figure after figure emerges from the crypt and corridors, where they had loitered in

the gloom; they assemble round the sarcophagus, which sheds from within a pale, unearthly light upon the silent awe-struck beings that surround it. Fair and lovely they appear, the sons and daughters of a high-born race, exempt from the common evils of life, but awake to all its generous sensibilities and higher perceptions. Pensive is every countenance, and soft is every falling footstep; yet in gentle accents many a voice breathes thanks to him who hath rolled back the current of time to show them glorious visions of the past, yet taught them to feel, even in the hour of pleasure itself, that "The paths of glory lead but to the grave." Such, I believe, were the feelings of all who had the gratification of witnessing the most impressive scene in the year 1825, when Sir John Soane had it thus prepared for three evenings, during which the rank and talent of this country, to an immense number, including many foreigners of distinction, enjoyed an exhibition as striking as it must ever be unrivalled. Had any one of that gay company been placed alone in the sepulchral chamber, at the "witching hour of night," when "Churchyards yawn and give up their dead," when the flickering lights become self-extinguished, and the last have been affected with the darker train of emotions which a situation so unallied to common life is calculated to produce. The awe ameliorated by beauty, and softened by tender reminiscence, would be exchanged for the mysterious expectation of some terrific visitant from the invisible world; and the very strongest mind would explain with Hamlet:– "There are more things in heaven and earth, Horatio, Than are dreamt of in your philosophy."' [29]

It has been speculated that the celebrations that Soane so carefully orchestrated to welcome the sarcophagus in 1825 and which are so powerfully evoked by Mrs Hofland, with her emphasis on the actual experience of an individual making his or her way through the museum, had something of the quality of an initiation about them and were no less than an attempt to recreate the spirit of the ancient 'Eleusian mysteries' in Lincoln's Inn Fields during which new truths could suddenly become visible, especially to those initiates of 'generous sensibilities and higher perceptions'.[30]

Helen Dorey

The sarcophagus lit by candles from within at night, detail of the west end.

NOTES

1 Belzoni's *Narrative of the Operations and Recent Discoveries within the pyramids, temples, tombs, and excavations, in Egypt and Nubia; and of a journey to the coast of the Red Sea, in search of the ancient Berenice; and another to the oasis of Jupiter Ammon*, 1820, as quoted by Soane in his 1835 *Description of the Residence of Sir John Soane . . .*, p.33

2 *Diana*, despite her English-sounding name, was a Turkish frigate. The ship was owned by Mehmet Ali Pasha of Egypt and was coming to England to be refitted for the Pasha after negotiations between the Admiralty and Briggs & Co. (fascinating in light of the fact that war was beginning with Greece – there was obviously a political dimension). Contemporary newspapers recorded that she had on board her a sarcophagus for the exhibition by Belzoni of his Egyptian expeditions. I am grateful to Jeremy Michell of the Historic Photographs and Ship Plans collections at the National Maritime Museum for drawing this to my attention (the NMM holds plans of *Diana* taken in 1821 at Deptford: object ID ZAZ2340)

3 For a more detailed account of Belzoni's discoveries and Salt's involvement, see Stanley Mayes, *The Great Belzoni*, 1959 and Deborah Manley and Peta Ree, *Henry Salt: Artist, Traveller, Diplomat, Egyptologist*, 2001

4 SM Library 1675

5 Soane's *Notebooks* are part of the Soane Archive, kept at the Museum, and cover the period 1781–1835

6 Susan M. Pearce, 'Giovanni Battista Belzoni's exhibition of the reconstructed tomb of Pharaoh Seti I in 1821', *Journal of the History of Collections* 12 no. 1 (2000), pp. 109–125. Soane's purchase of a single lot (no. 42 – 'A very fine Specimen of the Neck and Cover to a Jug ...') at the dispersal sale of Belzoni's Egyptian Hall exhibits pre-dates by almost two years his spectacular acquisition of the alabaster sarcophagus in May 1824 (see Stanley Mayes, *The Great Belzoni*, 1959, p. 275)

7 SM Library PC 118/17

8 SM Archive Priv. Corr. II. T. 13.1

9 All his correspondence is in the Soane Archive in a box compiled by Walter Spiers (Curator 1904–17)

10 Soane's volumes of newspaper cuttings cover the years 1767–1836 and are part of the Soane Archive

11 John Soane, *Description of the House and Museum of John Soane, Architect*, 1830, p. 9

12 Sir John Soane's Museum is a web of allusions and associations that can be read as a series of shrines to those admired by its creator throughout time. See Helen Dorey, 'Death and Memory: the Architecture of Legacy in Sir John Soane's Museum' in *Death and Memory, Soane and the Architecture of Legacy*, exhibition catalogue, 2015

13 *The Times*, December 11, 1824

14 This correspondence is in the Spiers box in the Soane Archive op. cit. note 6

15 SM Archive 7/7/46 and 7/8/35–36

16 This information comes from the *Day Books* in which Soane's pupils recorded their activities each day (Soane Archive)

17 John Soane, *Description of the House and Museum of John Soane . . .*, 1830, p. 2

18 The *Pasticcio* was taken down in 1896 because it was unsafe but was reinstated in 2004

19 Interestingly, there was no permanent hanging light in this position and the Picture Room had no fixed lighting at all, according to all the watercolour views of it from Soane's time and the inventory of fittings and fixtures compiled on his death, which records only one hanging lamp in the entire house, in the Monk's Parlour. This may have been because of the challenges that would have been involved in accessing and servicing such lights in Soane's interiors on a daily basis

20 The Monk's Parlour and the Picture Room, directly above it, were constructed in 1824

21 *The Crayon*, Vol. 1, No. 22 (May 30, 1855), pp. 341–343

22 SM Archive Priv. Corr. I.A.3.2

23 Robert Peel (later Sir Robert; 1788–1850), at this time
Home Secretary (an office he held from 1822 to 1827)
in Lord Liverpool's government. Interestingly, he later
opposed the Soane Museum Act in 1833

24 Bernardino de la Trinidad González Rivadavia y
Rivadavia (1780 –1845) later became the first President of
Argentina, then called the United Provinces of Rio de la
Plata, from February 1826 to July 1827. At the time of the
sarcophagus party he was Minister of State for Buenos
Aires under its Governor. He was responsible for the
construction of many of its grand avenues and schools and
for the foundation of its university and many museums

25 SM Archive Priv. Corr. II.S.28.3

26 Stanley Mayes, *The Great Belzoni*, 2003, p. 268

27 Despite his presence at this reception Soane owned only
one work by the poet Samuel Taylor Coleridge (1772–
1834): the short poem *The Devil's Walk* (an 1830 edition).
For Soane's close friendship with the artist Joseph Mallord
William Turner (1775–1851) see Helen Dorey, *John Soane
and J.M.W Turner: illuminating a friendship*, exhibition
catalogue, Sir John Soane's Museum, 2007

28 Eric George, *The Life and Death of Benjamin Robert Haydon*,
1948, p. 139

29 Sir John Soane, *Description of the Residence of John Soane . . .,*
1835, pp. 38–39

30 Gregory Dart, 'A Cockney Eleusis' in Chapter 6, 'John
Martin, John Soane and Cockney Art', Gregory Dart
(ed.), *Metropolitan Art and Literature, 1810–1840, Cockney
Adventures,* pp. 194–202. Professor Dart notes that
Soane's friend the auctioneer James Christie voiced deep
regret that he wouldn't be able to attend the nocturnal
exhibition, not least because it would have fitted so well
with his sense of the lamplight ceremonies that had taken
place at Eleusis

INDEX   Page numbers in *italic* refer to the illustrations

PICTURE CREDITS AND ACKNOWLEDGEMENTS

A.C. Cooper Limited. By courtesy of the Trustees of Sir John Soane's Museum: front cover, frontispiece, 6, 30 (left), 36, 40, 41, 44, 47, 48, 50, 51, 53, 55, 61, 63, 65, 67, 69, 71, 73, 74 (below), 87, 88, 91

Ardon Bar-Hama. By courtesy of the Trustees of Sir John Soane's Museum: front flap, back cover, 12, 15, 16, 17, 18, 19, 21

John Bridges. By courtesy of the Trustees of Sir John Soane's Museum: 31

© The Trustees of the British Museum: back flap, 11, 13, 32, 35

Lewis Bush. By courtesy of the Trustees of Sir John Soane's Museum: 30 (above)

Graham Harrison: 27

The Daniel Katz Gallery, London: 3

Reproduced by permission of Katz Pictures Limited from Leonard Cottrell, *The Warrior Pharaohs*, London 1968, plate 24 (The Mansell Collection): 29

Metropolitan Museum of Art, Rogers Fund, 1922 (22.2.21). © 2017. Image copyright The Metropolitan Museum of Art/ Art Resource/ Scala, Florence: 22

Monika Polak. By courtesy of the Trustees of Sir John Soane's Museum: 20 (right)

By courtesy of Belinda Rathbone: 20 (left)

By courtesy of the Trustees of Sir John Soane's Museum: 8, 81, 83, 85, 86

John H. Taylor: 9

Claire Thorne: 9 (above), 10 (right), 23 and the diagrams of the surfaces of the sarcophagus illustrating the location of the sections of the *Book of Gates* in the Chapter on the Decoration of the Sarcophagus (pp. 37-74)

Werner Forman Archive: 43, 74 (above)

John Williams. By courtesy of the Trustees of the British Museum: 24-6

Sir John Soane's Museum is very grateful to Alexandra Epps for her help with the picture research for this book.